The Disappearance of Evelyn Hartley

Kristin Morton

Published by Trellis Publishing, 2021.

While every precaution has been taken in the preparation of this book, the publisher assumes no responsibility for errors or omissions, or for damages resulting from the use of the information contained herein.

THE DISAPPEARANCE OF EVELYN HARTLEY

First edition. July 15, 2021.

Copyright © 2021 Kristin Morton.

ISBN: 979-8224568833

Written by Kristin Morton.

The Disappearance of Evelyn Hartley

Kirstin Morton

The scene is a peaceful suburban setting in an area where trouble rarely calls. Excitement fills the air as a big community event ensues, but in one house there is a studious babysitter quietly reading her books while the radio plays softly and the children in their charge sleeps peacefully upstairs. Nothing seems out of the ordinary until the sitter meets a terrifying and untimely end at the hands of a deranged, usually masked, villain. It's become something of a trope in horror movies over the decades, with gargantuan figures, such as Michael Myers from the infamous *Halloween* franchise, preying upon unsuspecting teenagers in unfamiliar locations at the dead of night. But for one teenage girl and her family, this nightmare would become a reality.

Evelyn Grace Hartley was the youngest of four children. Born on November 21, 1937, she lived happily with her family in La Crosse County, Wisconsin. She was an intelligent and caring girl. As a junior at Central High School in 1953, fifteen-year-old Evelyn was an A-grade student who participated in many of the extra-curricular activities the school offered. She had a particular interest in music, was a skilled pianist, and sang in her church's choir every Sunday. Dedicated to her local church, she volunteered as an Officer at the Presbyterian Youth Program and Westminster Fellowship. Evelyn was loving and well-liked, but was known for preferring study over play, favouring a night in with her books over large social events. This was the reason Evelyn accepted a babysitting job at 2415 Hoeschler Drive on Saturday October 24, 1953.

Viggo Rasmusen worked with Evelyn's father, Richard Hartley, as a professor at La Crosse State College. He was in need of a stand-in babysitter for that particular Saturday evening in October, as his usual sitter, Janice Lucille Cowley, had plans to attend the homecoming game at the school the same evening. Rasmusen also wanted to attend the event to cheer on his La Crosse State College students as they faced their competitors, River Falls. Knowing Evelyn to be a responsible girl in Cowley's class at school, Viggo approached Richard with the idea that Evelyn look after his twenty-month-old daughter, also named Janice. Richard discussed the idea with his daughter, and true to her reliable and responsible nature, Evelyn accepted. Before being picked up by Viggo at 6.30pm, she packed a bag with a variety of school books, planning to study while the baby slept, and promised her father that she would call at 8.30pm to let him know everything was going well. But the phone did not ring at the Hartley residence that night.

Richard Hartley began to worry as 8.30pm passed with no news from his daughter. It was out of character for Evelyn to break her word. Richard tried calling the Rasmusen house several times to no avail. At 9.20pm, he decided to drive to the house and check in on his daughter in person. There was no answer when he arrived and rang the doorbell, causing him further concern. All of the lights appeared to be on in the house and he could hear the faint sound of the radio playing, yet there was no sound of movement. Making his way around the outside of the house, he found all of the doors were locked. Eventually able to enter the building, he was confronted with every parent's worst nightmare: the scene of a violent struggle.

The Rasmusen's living room was in disarray, with the furniture upturned and moved to different parts of the room. Evelyn's school books were scattered across the floor. Her eyeglasses and one of her shoes were laying discarded in the living room, alongside footprints from a pair of sneakers. Panicked, Richard searched the house to try and find his daughter. He found various household items strewn around the home. Checking the baby's room, Richard saw that Janice lay asleep in her crib, but there was no sign of Evelyn anywhere in the house. Pry marks were found at three of the home's windows, but all entry points to the newly developed home were locked and secure, except from the basement at the back of the house. Making his descent into the lower part of the house, Richard found Evelyn's other shoe. He then discovered an open window in the basement with the screen missing, later to be discovered leaning against an outside wall. Another set of footprints made by sneakers were visible in the window box. Positioned by the open window was a small stepladder the Rasmusens had been using while painting their new home, and on the floor was a horrifying pool of blood. The blood trail continued outside, with two large pools found in the yard, further blood stains on the walls of a neighbour's house, and a bloody handprint approximately four feet off of the ground on a garage wall just down the street from the Rasmusen home.

At approximately 9.49pm, Richard rushed across the street to Frank Linder's home and urged him to call the police. Authorities quickly arrived on the scene and began their investigation. Finding footprints similar to those in and around the Rasmusen home in various areas around the neighbourhood, police suggested that the kidnapping wasn't predetermined, although there is debate as to whether or not the attacker saw Evelyn enter the house. A botched robbery was also discounted as a motive, as nothing of value was taken from the home. The police determined that the attacker must have carried Evelyn across the yard, putting her down at the two scenes where blood had collected. Aghast at the sight of these blood pools, Evelyn's mother, Ethel, was reportedly convinced that her daughter was dead at the scene of the crime. However, investigating officers speculated that the blood wasn't an indicator of fatal injuries, instead suspecting that it may have been caused by a bloody nose. They used bloodhounds to track Evelyn's scent, following a trail that led for two blocks, stopping at Coulee Drive, With the trail ending so suddenly, the authorities believed that she was likely placed in a vehicle and driven away. This theory was reiterated by information from local man, Ed Hofer. On October 26, Hofer approached the authorities, stating his vehicle was nearly hit by a speeding two-tone green Buick at roughly 7.15pm on the night of the incident. He saw three figures in the car: one male in the driver's seat, another male in in back, and a girl, slumped forward with her head against the front seat's headrest.

Initially assuming the trio were heading to the homecoming game, Hofer didn't think anything of it, and left the Buick to continue its drive westward. It wasn't until he heard the news of Evelyn's disappearance the next day that he realised the significance of what he had witnessed.

As locals continued to come forward with information, the homecoming game would prove to have repeatedly prevented Evelyn's chances of receiving help from anyone nearby. Nearby neighbours, Elvin and Helen Saterback, told the police they had heard two or three concerning screams at approximately 7pm, with the final scream sounding as if it had been cut short. The witnesses assumed the noise was just rowdy children carried away by the excitement of the game, and the abrupt end to the last cry had been caused by the child being taken indoors to be scolded by parents. Helen admitted she thought the screaming sounded like cries telling someone to "stop" or "get away". Similarly, a passer-by told the police that he had witnessed two young men dragging an apparently dazed young female along, but once again assumed it was just youngsters who had been carried away by the celebrations, drinking too much. The collective evidence allowed police to deduce that Evelyn had been abducted at approximately 7pm, meaning the incident happened early into her babysitting shift, as the Rasmusens had left for the game at 6.45pm. Further bad news was delivered to the police as the FBI informed John Bosshard, the La Cross County District Attorney, that they would not get involved in the case, claiming the initial evidence presented did not suggest the crime scene was one of a federal offense, ultimately deeming it a sex crime rather than kidnap or murder.

While the FBI rebuffed Evelyn and the Hartley family, La Crosse County saw the biggest search party in the state of Wisconsin continue to grow. Regular radio bulletins were aired, urging people to volunteer their time to look for the missing girl. As word spread, locals rushed to the area offering to help. It was estimated that at least 1,000 people joined the search within the first 24 hours, including representatives from the Naval Reserve, the Army Reserve, the Auxiliary Police Force, Wisconsin's National Guard, and Boy Scouts, as well as staff and students from La Crosse State College where Richard Hartley and Viggo Rasmusen worked. The nearby rivers were routinely dragged, and the Civil Air Patrol searched from the air, regularly volunteering their resources to the search, flying from Winona, Minnesota, to Stoddard, Wisconsin, while the Air Force also deployed helicopters to scan the area. Hunters were asked to keep an eye open while trekking the woods. Evelyn's brother, Thomas, repeatedly drove the family car along nearby highways in hope of finding some trace of his sister. The community raised funds to enable the Hartley family to offer a reward for any information, amounting to an impressive total of $6,600, which would be just under $61,000 today. The *La Crosse Tribune* reported on October 26, "Saturday night was a sleepless one for the girl's parents ... their family as well as the Rasmusens. It didn't matter to the Rasmusens that thousands trampled their recently sodded lawn around the beautiful new home. They knew the majority of the folks had come out to lend a friendly hand." Indeed, the La Crosse County police department were criticised for allowing so many citizens into the crime scene so soon after the event, fearing evidence may have been tampered with. Nevertheless, people continued to help, and the police remained very open with their investigation.

A few days later, the police uncovered a pair of pants and a brassiere lying at the side of the road near the underpass on Highway 14, just two miles south of Evelyn's home town. Four miles further along the highway, a bloodstained pair of men's pants were found. Whether the three items of clothing were connected remains inconclusive, but the blood on the clothing matched Evelyn's blood type. Soon after, on November 19, the police followed a lead having been tipped off by various farmers. They had each driven past the same peculiar items in the Coon Valley area to the southeast of La Crosse, and reported them to the police. Lying by the side of the road was a pair of size eleven Goodrich sneakers, and just 800 feet away from the shoes was a tired size 36 denim jacket, covered in blood on the front, back, and sleeves. Once again, the blood matched Evelyn's type. Authorities were encouraged by this discovery, considering the shoes to be "the most important pieces of evidence we have in the abduction of fifteen-year-old Evelyn Hartley." The police believed the shoes had been abandoned at the side of the highway shortly before they were found, perhaps as a distraction technique. Upon closer inspection of the items, police discovered the sneakers' soles had a suction-cup pattern which closely matched the footprints at the crime scene. There was also a distinctive wear pattern on the soles which led experts to conclude that the owner regularly rode a Whizzer motorbike. Reaching out to the Goodrich company, they were able to determine the name of the particular style of shoe, "Hood Mogul", and the states they were sold in, helping to narrow the search. Furthermore, each of these shoes had a serial number, which the police used in attempt to trace the owner. However, it was possible the shoes were second hand. This make of shoe hadn't been sold in the Wisconsin area for nearly three years, and experts suggested that two different people had worn the shoes, being too small for the second wearer. The jacket also had distinctive features, with metallic buttons and a strip cut from the bottom and roughly re-hemmed. A well-worn print into the fabric of the jacket suggested that the owner of the clothing may have worked as a steeplejack. Certain these items had been worn by Evelyn's abductor, the police travelled to 31 different communities in the Wisconsin area, showing the shoes and jackets to the public. Although more than 10,000 people were exposed to these pieces of evidence, no one recognised them, proving to be a devastating blow to the one promising lead authorities had uncovered.

Thorough investigations continued throughout La Crosse County's surrounding community. A sticker campaign was launched on October 29th. Police Chief George Long was intent on searching all of the cars in the county, and ordered gas station attendants to check vehicles for bloodstains. Searched cars which turned no evidence were given a sticker which read "My Car is OK". Over 40,000 of these stickers were printed. Any drivers who refused the inspection had to be reported to the police. Fresh graves were even reopened to ensure Evelyn's remains had not been hidden alongside a recent burial. With few clues coming to light, authorities took drastic measures and began conducting mass polygraphing, intending to test all the high school boys in the area to see if they knew anything about the disappearance. The *La Crosse Tribune* stated that the police were able to test four boys within an hour on the first day of testing, asking just five simple questions to each interviewee. Unfortunately, the testing proved too controversial within the community, and was halted after only 300 participants had cleared the polygraph.

It has been estimated that during the first year of Evelyn's disappearance, over 2,000 people helped in the search, making it the largest ever of its kind in Wisconsin. Police claim that during that same time period, they questioned over 3,500 people in connection with the disappearance. Unfortunately, their diligent searching turned no leads, leaving the Hartley family heartbroken and hopeless. Her father openly appealed for information regularly, urging the abductor to come forward, "I know that the police department and the other authorities are doing everything possible with the meagre information they have to find Evelyn or her abductor ... Of course, the person who has the most information is the abductor. I am appealing to him to reveal the location of Evelyn or her body. I do not expect him to reveal his identity. But he can give us something to lead us to the girl."

The authorities received many dead-end leads and false confessions following Evelyn's abduction. Shortly after the news of Evelyn's disappearance broke, a woman in Madison, Wisconsin, requested that police arrest her fifteen-year-old son in relation to the case. The boy had run away from his home in May 1953, returned home for a few days, and left again on October 24th. He reappeared in early November to collect some of his clothing and possessions, where he told his mother that he knew Evelyn and had dated her. Upon receiving this tip, police rushed from La Crosse County to Madison to take the boy in for questioning, but were ultimately left with little evidence that he had been involved in the case. In fact, Richard Hartley was insistent that he had never met the boy, and the family's relationship was so open that he would have been aware of any boyfriends Evelyn might have had. Although she had been on a few dates, she had never been courted by a boy long-term. A local man named Jack Duffrin also claimed to have information about the case. The twenty-year-old called the Hartley family twice in response to their public appeals for information. Each time, he offered to exchange key information in return for $500. Working together, the Hartleys and the authorities set up a trap for Duffrin and caught both the suspect and a thirteen-year-old boy. Proving to have no real knowledge about the case, Duffrin was ultimately arrested, convicted, and imprisoned for extortion.

The police also closely interrogated recently arrested criminals in hopes of gaining any clues. It was estimated that seventy-five sex offenders were questioned and cleared of involvement. Forty-three-year-old Bernard J Lauer was held on a rape charge shortly after the incident. The salesman, originally from Eau Claire, was in the area selling roofing in late October 1953, but he had a reliable alibi for the night of Evelyn's disappearance. A twenty-year-old man, Robert Snodgrass, was questioned in the days following the abduction. He had been arrested for indecent exposure, but his alibi for the evening was also solid. Another young man, John Mulqueen, was arrested after confessing to the murder of an army captain near Menomonie. Once again, there was no evidence to link Mulqueen to Evelyn's abduction, and upon tracing activity on his gasoline credit card, it was revealed he was in Houston on October 24th. Hayverd Tygue became another suspect in the case. The nineteen-year old had been arrested for driving a stolen car from his home city of Chicago to Wisconsin. As he was questioned, details of further crimes became apparent, bearing striking similarities to Evelyn's case. Tygue had attacked two women in Madison. In one instance, he broke into a house in a newly developed neighbourhood by entering through the basement window. He attacked his unsuspecting victims with a baton, but fled each time when the women began screaming. Police searched the car in question, a tan colour vehicle with Illinois license plates. It appeared to match the description a neighbour provided of a car circling the neighbourhood three times at roughly 8pm the evening before Evelyn was taken. The police also found a lead pipe with human hairs on it in the vehicle. Tygue was ultimately questioned, but once again lead to a dead-end for police, as he was not in La Crosse on the night of October 24th.

Perhaps the most notorious criminal linked to the case was Ed Gein. Known as the Butcher of Plain Field, Gein was a murderer and body snatcher who used his victim's skin and bones to make stomach-churning trophies which police found in his house. His disturbed mind has been forever immortalized in fiction and popular culture, influencing the creation of characters such as Norman Bates in Robert Bloch's novel and Alfred Hitchcock's silver screen adaptation, *Psycho*, and Leatherface in movie franchise, *The Texas Chainsaw Massacre*. Following his arrest, it was discovered that he was in La Crosse County at the time of Evelyn's disappearance, and he happened to be visiting a relative who lived just a few blocks away from the Rasmusen residence. Denying any involvement, Gein took two lie detector tests in relation to Evelyn's case, but passed them both. Police searched Gein's house of horrors for any evidence, but found nothing that suggested Evelyn had fallen victim to Gein. In November 1957, Gein was publicly cleared of any involvement in the case. Considered legally insane, Gein spent the rest of his life in a mental institution. His involvement in the case is still debated today, as his presence in

La Crosse during the time of the disappearance seems too coincidental to some, while his unstable mental state could potentially make his testimony and any test results unreliable. However, it would also have been out of character for Gein to work with an accomplice, and it seems unlikely that he would have broken his pattern of keeping trophies.

The case gained such notoriety in the area, that people continued to provide false confessions decades after the event. In 1971, a fifty-one-year-old transient man named Tommy Thompson was arrested in Casper, Wyoming for cashing bad checks. During his questioning, he claimed that he had kidnapped, raped, and murdered a fifteen-year-old babysitter in La Crosse County in 1953. Police investigated further, but found Thompson was serving time in a Minnesota prison during the time of the abduction. Instead, he was charged for making a false statement. Further evidence was revealed in 2004, when police finally hoped they had caught the break they were looking for, fifty years after Evelyn went missing. While researching a book about the case, Andy Thompson, Peggy Lovejoy, and Susan T. Hessel's investigation triggered a memory for Wisconsin man, Mel Williams. In 1968, Williams was recording in The Raven, a bar in La Forge. At the time, he was a musician and would regularly tape bands playing. A visitor to the area, Williams wanted to get some of the local characters on tape, and was drawn to one man in particular, telling the *La Crosse Tribune* in 2004, "This (man) was quite a character, buying booze for a bunch of alcoholic friends. I wanted him on tape for the memory." The character turned out to be Clyde Tywee Peterson, and he was standing at the bar with a man named Whitey Barclay. In the recording, the pair clearly allude to Evelyn's abduction. In the released transcription, Barclay can be heard to say, "That's ... about the time you hauled that Hartley girl down there ... That right?" The men continued to discuss the disappearance, referring to the police searching graves and repeatedly naming the Hartley family, with Barclay going so far as to say, "You know damn right he all done it … and I know it, and he told me with his own mouth." In the recording, they implicate a man named Jack Gaulthair, and reveal that his role in the abduction drove him to suicide. Indeed, it was publicly reported that Gaulthair had taken his own life on Christmas Day, 1967. The recording ends with Barclay stating his theories on where Evelyn's body might be buried and mentioning another unnamed man who might know what really happened to her, before turning to Williams and demanding he stop the tape, "shut it off, shut it off!" The County Sheriff in place in 2004 was Gene Carey, who agreed that this discovery could prove vital to the case. Unfortunately, being so many years after the recording was made, this new lead failed to open any new doors.

Sixty-five years later, the tragic disappearance of Evelyn Hartley still remains unsolved. Her parents eventually moved to Oregon to be close to their daughter, Carolyn, ultimately accepting that it was unlikely their youngest child would ever be found. The abductor remains unmasked, and the case continued to haunt the Rasmusen family, who moved to a new home soon after Evelyn's abduction. Speaking with the La Crosse Tribune on the twenty-fifth anniversary of the event, Viggo Rasmusen stated the whole experience continued to be "a nightmare, whenever we think of it. I don't mean it preys on our minds constantly, but we don't forget it no matter how long ago it was." Their daughter, Janice, grew up with a detailed knowledge of the case, but no memory of the events. As an active baby, her parents were always thankful that she slept quietly and peacefully on the night of October 24th, not alerting the criminal to her presence in the house. The disappearance demonstrated the true power of community. The vast number of volunteers and the generous donations locals made to the case was astounding. Even four years after her abduction, 84-year-old Howard George spent the little money he had to hire private investigators from the Hargrave Secret Services for three months to help with the case. Unfortunately, by the time they had completed their report, they had compiled no new evidence or leads, and Howard had passed away. In a devastating case haunted by continuous dead-ends, false confessions, and no closure, lies the heart of a dedicated community committed to ensuring Evelyn's memory lives on.

finding jodi

CHRISSY THOMPSON

Jodi Sue Huisentruit was a news anchor for KIMT, a station based in Mason City, Iowa. On June 27th, 1995, she called the station and told her co-worker that she was on her way to work after she overslept.

It would be the last time anyone heard from her.

There were signs of a struggle outside of her apartment indicating that she had been abducted. She would disappear without a trace. Numerous rumors and "persons of interest" have emerged but no official suspect has ever been named.

Over twenty years later, the question still remains.

What happened to Jodi Huisentruit?

EARLY LIFE

Jodi was born in Long Prairie, Minnesota, the youngest daughter of Maurice Huisentruit and Imogene "Jane" Huisentruit. Her father would pass away at age sixty-two of colon cancer. Jodi was only fourteen at the time.

Jodi was an excellent student who also excelled at golf. She would lead her high school team to victory in the state Class A tournament in 1985 and 1986. After high school, she would attend St. Cloud State University where she majored in TV Broadcasting and Speech Communication.

After graduating college, she worked for Northwest Airlines as a stewardess until she landed her first broadcasting gig at KGAN in Cedar Rapids, Iowa. She then briefly returned to Minnesota to work at KSAX before relocating to Iowa for a job at KIMT.

Jodi was well-liked at the station and immediately became a hit with her viewers who liked the infectious enthusiasm of the sunny blonde. She was petite, blonde and had a made for television smile.

Family members, however, would often worry about Jodi as they perceived her as a bit naïve.

"She would befriend anyone," investigative reporter Steve Powell said. "It was part of her nature and that is what made her a popular fixture at the station. In some of her family home videos, you can see the playfulness of her nature. She was outgoing and bubbly. Not the type of person who made enemies."

"I hired Jodi," said Doug Merbach, former news director of KIMT. "I brought her to Mason City. Could there have been something we could have warned her about and talked to her about? I don't know. What do you think happened? I've been asked that so many times. I feel as ignorant as the next person. I just don't know. I don't want to point fingers at anybody without looking inside the investigation and opening up those books. I don't know. I think it had to be somebody who knew her. I think it had to be somebody who had an emotional response to something Jodi said or did that caused them to do that. I don't think it was random - I don't think it was planned. I think it was planned to a certain extent - but not days and weeks ahead of time."

"She had so much enthusiasm," her best friend at the station, Robin Woflram said. "Every day was a gift and treated as something to explore. Sometimes occasionally she would call, I mean this girl got up at 3 am, and she said 'What are you doing after work?' It's like 10:30 pm and I'd tell her that I'm going home and going to bed. She'd say, 'Oh, Robin, there's plenty of time to sleep. Life is for the living.' And she embraced every single moment."

"It's sometimes difficult to get close - especially women - in this industry because you're always looking over your shoulder and wondering if someone is coming up behind me. I'll never forget the first day she walked in and her laugh. She'll always be remembered for that. She's fun and spunky. I think I'll like her. She's got zest for living."

JODI IS MISSING

Huisentruit would play in a golf tournament the day before she disappeared. She then went to the home of John Vansice and according to him, they watched a videotape of her birthday party that he had arranged for her.

On June 27th, 1995, KIMT producer Amy Kuns noticed that Jodi still had not reported for work. She called her at the apartment and explained that she had overslept.

"I'm on my way," Jodi said.

Two hours later, Jodi still had not arrived at the station.

Kuns would substitute for her on her morning show Daybreak.

An hour later, she would call the Mason City police.

"It became known only after that Jodi wasn't always punctual," Powell said. "A lot of her co-workers covered for her because they didn't want her to get in trouble with the brass at the station. So, her arriving late wasn't that much of an unusual occurrence. Not showing up at all certainly was, however, and they called for the police to do a welfare check."

Police would arrive at Jodi's apartment and find her red Mazda Miata still parked in the apartment lot. There was evidence suggesting that there had been a struggle near her car.

Jodi's keys were stuck in the driver side door, broken in half. Her blow dryer, jewelry, and red high heels were strewn about in the parking lot.

The top of her convertible was dented. Blood and tissue was splattered on the driver side mirror. Skid marks on the pavement suggested that she had been dragged to a waiting vehicle."

"The scene suggested that she had been grabbed while putting her keys in the car door," Powell said. "She was in a rush, having overslept for whatever reason. Was probably going to make herself up on the way to the station when someone rushed up behind her."

There was a palm print left behind on her car which police were never able to identify.

MORNING SCREAMS

Police would inquire with neighbors and found three tenants who stated that they heard screams in the early morning hours. Another neighbor reported seeing a white van with lights on parked nearby Jodi's vehicle.

Three months after her disappearance, Jodi's family would hire private investigators from McCarthy and Associates (MAIS) in Minneapolis who then worked in tandem with another private investigator, Doug Jasa.

"A lot of things struck me about the case," Jasa said. "I still remember all of the cards they found in Jodi's apartment. They were birthday cards. I think there were 50 of them and we're reading through them - reading through them. People had written very nice notes in the birthday cards. We went door to door in the apartment complex - talking with different residences about what they heard. One lady remembers specifically looking at her clock when she heard the scream."

Her family held out hope throughout the harrowing ordeal.

"I couldn't have had a better kid sister," Jodi's older sister Joanne Nathe said. "She tried to motivate me. What are your goals? That makes me stronger. It's a nightmare...not knowing where she is. We were hoping to find her in the first few months."

Neither the police nor the private investigators would come up with any evidence. All they had were more questions.

Questions that would forever remain unanswered.

"What caused her to sleep in that day," Officer Terrance Prochaska with Mason City Police Department asked. "What caused her to answer the phone and rush into work? What was she doing the night before? We all want to know the fine details. We know where she was at. She was golfing. She had driven home and made a phone call to her friend. Those are facts. But its' that gray area in between that we don't understand."

Rumors would plague the investigation as numerous false hopes and bizarre allegations were made. Mason City had a growing drug problem and some speculated that Jodi was working on a story to expose drug dealers. This was an outlandish claim considering that

Jodi was not an investigative reporter and was not trained for that discipline. KIMT was a call-in television station. They got their news from the wires and reported it after some fact-checking. Another unfounded rumor came from a disgruntled female police officer who claimed that two of her fellow officers were responsible for Jodi's disappearance. Again, these were uncorroborated allegations and the officer spreading the rumors was terminated.

The community at large would get involved and in May of 1996, over one hundred volunteers searched the area of Cerro Gordo County. They would leave flags in the ground to mark anything they found to be suspicious. Authorities would then comb through the area but no further evidence was ever found.

Over one thousand interviews were conducted after her disappearance. Not one single suspect ever emerged.

Police initially turned their attention to the last person to have seen Jodi alive.

John Vansice.

Vansice was a lifelong Iowa native and lived in Newton where he was married with two children. He divorced in the early 1990s and moved to the Key Apartments in Mason City where he would befriend Jodi.

Jodi would reportedly spend a lot of time with the fifty-year-old Vansice. He was more than twenty years her senior and seemed to be "obsessed" with her. He threw around more money than his listed occupation (corn seeder) would suggest he could afford as he purchased a $26,000 boat in 1995 which he named "Jodi".

Jodi's purchase of the Mazda Miata seemed fishy as well as the car was more expensive than her meager salary as a broadcaster would allow.

STRANGER OR STALKER?

"I was the last to see her alive," Vansice said as he approached law enforcement officers investigating Jodi's apartment. He told police of what happened the night before, that Jodi was at his apartment watching a birthday video.

Vansice had taken special care in throwing Jodi a birthday party. He had printed out the invites himself, making sure his name was printed on the bottom with the words "a party given by John Vansice and friends."

Joann described Vansice as being "fixated" on her sister but stated that Jodi never mentioned anything about him during their conversations. She did mention Vansice in conversations with her mother and alluded to the fact that he may be developing a romantic interest in her. She also stated that she felt "uncomfortable" during a recent breakfast she had with Vansice.

Joann would describe a meeting she had with Vansice in which she thought his behavior was "cold" and "unfriendly." She asked Vansice if Jodi ever mentioned their Dad to him and he abruptly ended their conversation.

During his public appearances, Vansice seemed calm in relaying his support for Jodi's return.

Too calm.

"We're all praying and hoping that she's okay," Vansice said. "We just have to keep praying and keep hoping and I'll think she'll come back. I really do."

"I liked Jodi so much I named my boat after her," Vansice said when asked by a reporter why he named his boat after her. "She was such a big part of my life and she just made me feel so good."

Jodi's friend, Tammy Baker, once asked Jodi point blank if she was involved with Vansice.

"Absolutely not," Jodi said.

"Vansice was questioned by police but ruled out as he passed the lie detector tests," Powell said. "But any sociopath can pass a lie detector test. Vansice should have been suspect number one on the basis of telling the police that he 'was the last one to see her alive.' Making a statement like that, with no dead body found, is a revealing disclosure."

Most people close to the case believe that Vansice is involved but never directly say his name as if they are afraid.

"It is a head scratcher as to why the police didn't come at him harder," Powell said. "It was almost as if there was a veil of secrecy over his relationship with Jodi and what it exactly entailed. I believe that it may have been in part to protect Jodi's reputation. She was an All-American girl, church-raised and church-going. But the question had to be asked of what her relationship with Vansice exactly was or more specifically, what did he have in mind? Did he want to be her older sugar daddy? He bought her gifts, gave her birthday parties, making deposits in the account so to speak. But when he finally came to collect did she rebuff his advances and spur him to murderous anger?"

"What is certain is that he was her neighbor and they would hang out a lot. When they looked into her apartment they would find four cans of sixteen-ounce beers. No way the petite Jodi could handle that and then head off to work. The toilet seat was up. The other thing missing from her apartment was her personal notebook. Most sexual predators wouldn't steal something like that. But again, hindsight is 20/20 and they should have made a beeline for Vansice's boat the moment they found out that he named his boat after a woman whom he supposedly had a platonic relationship with."

THE DEATH OF A FRIEND

Three months prior to her disappearance, Jodi suffered the loss of a close friend named Billy Pruin. Pruin had just proposed to his girlfriend Gretchen Tusler and two days later he drove to Mason City to pick up a new tractor he had purchased. The next day, a friend went to his farmhouse and saw that his front door was ajar with the keys in the outside lock. He called out for his friend, received no answer, then he left.

No one had heard from Billy and then his mother went to his house to check on him. She would find him laying in a pool of blood, he had been shot in the chest.

Investigators listed his death as a suicide but later changed it to "undetermined".

His friends, Jodi included, could not believe that the jovial Billy committed suicide. He had just proposed to his girlfriend and bought a new tractor for a business. He had no reason to kill himself.

When Jodi disappeared, there was conjecture that the two deaths could be related.

His fiancee, Gretchen, was questioned after his death and stated that he often appeared "afraid of something" for weeks before his death.

Jodi voiced the same concerns prior to her disappearance. She written one of her best friends, Kelly Torgelson, revealing that "she was concerned for her safety, that she was being stalked."

Kelly would receive Jodi's letter in the mail on June 27th, 1995 at her home in Mississippi. The day that Jodi would be abducted.

"Jodi had reported that that a man in a pickup truck stopped and eyeballed her," Powell said. "This creeped her out. She felt as if someone was after her. So that is another theory that we have to go on in the case. Because of her position in the media and being a very attractive female, she was prone to have any nut ball start to fantasize and stalk her."

NO BODY, NO EVIDENCE

The investigators continued to grasp at straws while not pursuing anything against Vansice. They simply had nothing to pin him with.

Desperate for answers, the detectives and members of Jodi's family would meet with psychics in November of 1997.

"Psychics would be called upon a lot during the 1980s and 1990s," Powell said. "It was simply a sign of desperation from everyone involved. They needed anything, just anybody with some type of answer. So these charlatans would come in and they would go through the motions. When that happens, you know that the investigators have absolutely nothing."

Jodi's disappearance would leave her co-workers at KIMT devastated. Some left the business while others moved to other stations. Not one colleague that worked with Jodi during her tenure at KIMT remains with the station.

Wolfram, Jodi's friend and fellow broadcaster, would leave KIMT a few months after Jodi disappeared.

"They called me into the office and I thought they had found Jodi," Wolfram recalled. "Otherwise, why would all these people be in the office than to share that information. But there was talk on the internet - chat rooms - he claimed he knew who had abducted Jodi. Gruesome details. Then the reason they had brought me in was the last communication was that Robin Wolfram would be next. From that point on - I had a police escort at night. From that point forward, I look at life differently. I think I used to look at life in rose colored glasses and everyone had a pure heart like Jodi. I realized evil exists right next door to good. It's like a veil. You reach your hand across to experience it. And it's not that easy."

NEW LEADS, MORE FALSE HOPES

Jodi's case would remain in the public eye and garnered renewed interest on the 20th year anniversary of her disappearance.

In a bizarre twist, photocopies of Jodi's personal diary were anonymously mailed to a local newspaper in June of 2008. The journal was eighty-four pages long and sent to the Mason City Globe Gazette. The diary had been placed in a large envelope with no return address. Days later, however, the sender had come forward.

It was the wife of the former Mason City Police Chief.

Her motive for sending the copy to the newspaper remains unclear.

JODI'S JOURNAL

Jodi would start "journaling" after she purchased Anthony Robbins Success program.

Her entries would reveal some of her personal thoughts and how she prioritized things in terms of work, family, and friends. Throughout the pages, she expressed her love for travel, socializing and her search for someone to share her life with.

"Remember," one of her first entries read, "there is no time better than now to begin practicing being the best I can be and living the way I want to live."

Jodi would continue to write about her goals and desire to get the "Huisentruit name out." She listed Paula Zahn and Kathy Gifford as her role models.

She wrote about her dating life briefly, talking about male friends and her love for dancing. She had met a man she liked during a cruise she had taken with her mother. "Why do I get hooked so fast?" she asked in one entry. "I'm lonely here at times and would like to have someone to share my life with. Sure I meet men — but none that really strikes me, or who follows thru."

"My No. 1 goal is to get a new job," she wrote in April 1995, two months before her disappearance.

"I'm recovering from Memorial Day Weekend, unbelievable — Indy 500 — a time of my life. Partied with so many wonderful people — Mario Andretti (world class racer), Joe Dumars (Detroit Pistons basketball player) and Tim Allen (TV star from 'Home Improvement'). Had an incredible weekend."

The latter part of her entries focused more on her activities as opposed to her goals.

"I stayed in Mason City this weekend to regroup, gather my thoughts and goals, read! And have Jodi time. I've enjoyed it. Church is very important to me as is putting myself and family ... at the top. I'm starting fresh at work this week — getting up at 3 a.m. — best newscast in the world — top 10 market — I really think I'll market myself for AZ. — see what they think about my accent. Or I'll move down there to produce."

Her final three entries all mention John Vansice.

"What a weekend, Surprise," Jodi wrote on June 11, 1995. "My Mason City/Clear Lake friends thru a big party for me! At a lounge, wild. It was in Clear Lake. They had a 16 gal keg – huge cake (with a skier) so much left. John Van Sice grilled 150 pork burgers, we were dancing on tables...dancing everywhere...Everyone had a ball. Video camera was rolling, cameras were clicking – oh what fun! Life is so good. The party made me feel so good."

"Last night John,...and I went to the Glen Miller Orchestra in Belmond," Jodi wrote on June 13th, 1995. "I have so many great viewers. People are so kind. This nice weather has me wild. I bought a new Mazda Miata, simply love it."

"Got home from a weekend road trip to Iowa City," Jodi wrote in her final entry. "oh we had fun! It was wild, partying and water skiing. We skied at the Coralville Res. I'm improving on the skis — hips up, lean, etc. John's son Trent gave me some great ski tip advice. Today, Sunday, it was raining in Mason City so didn't get any skiing in. I love it, it's addicting." Later on in the entry she wrote about her desire to move on from KIMT. "Great friends but professionally, I'm fed up. It's difficult finding a new job and I'm confused about agent and what to do."

The journals didn't reveal any clues that furthered the investigation. It remains a head-scratcher as to why the wife of the former police chief would forward the journal to the newspaper.

"The journals said a lot about Jodi's character," Powell said. "Reading through it is heartbreaking because you realize how much she loved her life, her family, and friends. She was on the road to self-improvement and listened to Tony Robbins' success tapes. She aspired to beyond what she was doing. She wanted to make her mark."

NEW SUSPECT

One new suspect that did emerge in recent years was serial rapist Tony Dejuan Jackson. Jackson was twenty-one years old at the time of

Huisentruit's abduction and is now serving a life sentence in Minnesota for raping three women in 1997.

He was questioned about the crime and denied ever meeting Huisentruit or seeing her in public.

His former friend, however, stated otherwise.

Speaking anonymously, this friend would tell the Minneapolis news station KMSP that he had met Jackson because their girlfriends at the time were good friends. The source described an occasion where Jackson had invited him to get drinks where he knew Jodi was a regular.

The two then arrived at the South Bridge Lounge where they saw Jodi sitting at the bar.

He stated that Jackson walked right up to Jodi and began talking to her but he didn't hear the gist of their conversation.

Jackson was living in Mason City at the time and was attending North Iowa Community College. He hosted his own student talk show and wanted to pursue a career in broadcasting.

His friend thought that Jackson simply wanted to get career advice from Jodi not really thinking anything of their conversation until years later.

"My gut tells me that he probably did it," Jackson's friend said. "After all the stuff he's done since."

This suspicion of Jackson is corroborated with a neighbor who went out jogging early in the morning. She stated that the morning before she saw a young African American man, riding a bike outside the complex. He started biking ride beside her and she was spooked by him as it was so early in the morning.

Jackson would eventually be connected to over six sexual assaults on women from North Iowa to the St. Paul area in Minnesota.

He would arm himself with handcuffs, duct tape, mask and a gun as he stalked his victims. He threatened to kill his victims when they would not submit to him. One of his victims was eventually able to identify him as she worked with Jackson at a restaurant.

Jackson would write rap songs in prison that contained the lyric "stiffin' around Tiffin." Authorities believed that he may be referring to a silo in Tiffin, Iowa which he may have dumped her body. He had also told a cellmate that he was involved with a kidnapping of a news anchor.

Mason City police would not charge him, however, and it remains unclear why the eliminated him as a suspect.

As of this writing, John Vansice remains the primary person of interest. He has since moved to Phoenix, Arizona.

Jodi would be declared legally dead in May of 2001.

THE DISAPPEARANCE OF BRITTANEE DREXEL

28

FAITH TORINO

Brittanee Drexel disappeared from Myrtle Beach, SC while on spring break on April 25, 2009. She was 17 at the time and traveled without receiving parental consent. She told her mother that she was staying at a friend's house near their home in Rochester, New York. Brittanee's mother, Dawn, then learned where she really was when her boyfriend, John, called her after he suspected something had happened to Brittanee. Her parents immediately grew angry, scared, and devastated when they received word that their daughter was missing.

Brittanee was born on October 7th, 1991 and lived in Rochester, New York. She moved frequently during her youth as her father was in the military. She was a junior at Gates-Chili High school and the year was a rough one with her parents separating. She would live with her mother but still see her father frequently.

She was blind in her right eye and had several surgeries to correct her hyperplastic primary vitreous. To keep her eye from wandering, she would get contacts that made both eyes look the same.

Britt was described by friends and family as a smiling, fun-loving girl. Her demeanor had changed by her junior year in high school as she was depressed that her parents were separating. She would sleep in late and begin to skip school. She would overdose two times on her mother's pain medication and both times were fueled by the fact that she had just broken up with her on-again, off-again boyfriend, John Grieco.

"I felt it was all my fault," Brittany's father said. "When I was here none of this went on. She didn't ingest as many pills as they thought but still watching her get her stomach pumped was a warning. I need help."

"I remember the look on her face," Dawn said. "She was all red. She was crying, tears coming down her face. 'Why would you do this? Nothing in life is that bad.'"

Brittanee would be forced to see a counselor after the suicide attempt. Still, things seemed as if they were a mess on the home front.

Her parents were separating and her mother was losing her home. But she would resume her studies at school and excel on the soccer field.

"She was fast," her father said. "Her coach would say he'd never seen a girl that fast."

By the time Spring Break rolled around in, she was ready to go on an adventure with some of the older kids she knew. It was a long-standing tradition for Rochester students to go to Myrtle Beach for vacation. Britt wanted to enjoy the night life and lay out in the beach, so when one of her older friends asked if she wanted to come along she didn't hesitate.

She asked her mother first and the idea was immediately shot dawn. Dawn Drexel did not know any of the friends that would be taking Brittanee.

"She asked me and I said 'no,'" Dawn recalled. "Then she went to talk to her father. She would play us both. She would say Mom said 'no' but Dad said 'yes.'"

Brittanee was determined to go. She pleaded with her mother once again and was turned down. Angry, the two got into a fight and Britt would call her boyfriend to come pick her up.

Brittanee decided to fool her mother. She told her mother that she wanted to stay at a friend's house nearby for a couple of days. Dawn reluctantly agreed but Brittanee headed off to South Carolina instead.

Dawn believed that someone had offered her something, like a "modeling job or some other kind of ruse" to get her to go down there. She had aspirations of being a model as well as getting into cosmetology. With her striking good looks, she would be a shoo-in for success in the modeling profession.

"Her biological father was Turkish," Dawn said. "She had a very European look."

Defying her mother, Brittanee would visit her boyfriend at his workplace and tried to entice him to come along. The young man declined, stating that he had to work.

Brittanee then left with her older friends Jennifer Oberer, Phillip Oberer and Allana Lippa to Myrtle Beach. Jennifer was twenty-one years old. Her brother Phillip would be charged with rape in an unrelated case (charges would be dropped) in 2010. It is believed that these were considered the 'cool kids' and that Britt wanted to hang out and be liked by them.

Britt texted her boyfriend numerous times throughout the trip, telling him about the ambience. She expressed her love for the hot weather, palm trees and the happy vibe of young people finally away from parental supervision. But according to friends and family, Brittanee didn't know the older kids that well.

She also called her mother and lied, telling her that she waswatching movies at a friend's house.

CHANGE OF HEART

Britt hit the clubs with her friends and her mood quickly changed. Her friends began using a lot of drugs and she didn't want any part of that scene. She went off by herself, checking out the local shops and walking down the beach.

She then met up with a friend from Rochester, a man named Peter Brozowitz. He was also in town and staying at the Blue Water Resort with his own group of friends; Matthew Abrams, Philip Watson, Keith Cummings, and Anthony Schimizzi. The 20-year old Brozowitz was a "club promoter" who got Brittanee into Club Kryptonite. The next morning, she would meet Peter again at the beach.

The next day, Brittanee called her younger sister and told her that she's at the beach. Her sister believed she's at the local beach which is only twenty-minutes away. Britt then has a friend to impersonate the parent of the friend get on the phone to talk to her mother. The friend assured Dawn that everything was okay.

Britt then got back on the phone with her mother.

"I'll see you tomorrow," Britt said. "I love you and I'll see you tomorrow."

It would be the last time Dawn would ever speak to her daughter.

THE MYSTERY OF WHAT HAPPENED THAT NIGHT

Brittanee decided she would meet up with her friend Peter that night. She borrowed a pair of shorts from a friend and headed out. She texted her boyfriend John, telling him that she's having a miserable time and that she doesn't like the people she went down with. Apparently, they were 'mean-girling' her after she didn't do drugs with them.

She then received a text from her friend who stated that she wants her shorts back. Irritated, Brittanee walked back to the hotel to return the item.

At least that is what her friends say happened as Britt would disappear into the night.

John then became worried when Britt did not text him back. He texted her a few more times, waited, received no answer then he threatened to tell her mother that she's in South Carolina if she doesn't respond back.

Convinced that something is wrong, John calls Dawn at home. He explained that Brittanee is in Myrtle Beach.

Dawn went livid but her anger soon turned to concern when Britt didn't respond to her own texts or calls.

Everyone in Brittanee's family was notified. Something was wrong. Terribly wrong.

The next morning Dawn, her parents and John all made the trek to Myrtle Beach to try and look for Brittanee.

THE SEARCH BEGINS

Police in Myrtle Beach were notified and questioned the friends that Britt had been staying with. Their answers were all the same, they had not seen Brittanee since last night. Police also turned to Dawn, questioning her about Brittanee's state of mind.

Would she run away? Had she done this before?

There was no indication that Brittanee had motivation to do such a thing. Nor did they have any reason to believe she was doing a lot of drinking or drugs.

With no other leads, detectives turned their eyes on the last person to have seen Brittanee, Peter Brozovitz.

Peter would make an appearance on the Dr.Phil show and proclaim his innocence. He stated that they were in his hotel room watching the Yankees-Red Sox game when Brittanee was engaged in a texting argument with Jen Oberer who wanted her shorts back.

He said she didn't have a problem with walking a mile back to her own hotel.

Brittanee's parents were on the show and berated Peter for not "being a gentleman" and driving her back to the hotel. They also found it suspicious that Peter and the rest of Brittanee's friends did not do more after she was missing.

"I had spoken with Peter that morning," Dawn said. "He was giving me three different scenarios...It's fishy."

Peter responded angrily, stating that he was 'being thrown under the bus.' The innuendos were clear, that even if he had nothing to do with Brittanee's disappearance, she went missing because he didn't look out for her.

What is suspicious is that Peter had abruptly left Myrtle Beach with his friends around 2 a.m, five hours after Brittanee had vanished. They left clothing behind in their hotel room and looked to have been in a rush.

Upon his return to Rochester, Peter hired a defense attorney.

Peter had told investigators that she left his room shortly upon arrival to return the pair of shorts to her friend. The detectives got a hold of the surveillance camera from the hotel and verified Peter's story. At precisely 8:48 that evening she was seen leaving Peter's hotel to return back to her own hotel. She should have shown up on a traffic camera about fifteen minutes away but she never made it that far. She was abducted somewhere along that street.

Police continued to question Peter. The young man stated that one of his friends was told by his mother to return home immediately. This story was corroborated and law enforcement did not pursue the matter any further.

Instead, they now focused on Britt's cell phone.

Britt's last text message to her boyfriend was around 8:58. Ten minutes after she had left the hotel she texted "I'm packing and going to sleep probably."

This would be the last outbound message she sent as then John began texting her repeatedly with no answer back.

But the calls she received from John and her friends were pinged by her cell phone. Every time a friend called, her cell phone communicated with the nearest tower.

In looking at her cell phone records, she was moving southbound. The last ping was received at the Poleyard boat landing.

Fifty miles away from Myrtle Beach and two counties over.

Whoever abducted Brittanee knew exactly where they were going. The place was isolated, a rural country islet that only fishermen or locals would know about.

This was not the kind of place a seventeen-year-old girl would go to on Spring Break.

The investigators launched their search in the area that was about four miles in radius. Unfortunately, the terrain was treacherous. Alligators, wild hogs, snakes and biting insects the size of golf balls populated the area looking for their next meal.

Four-wheelers were brought in to keep the alligators away from the sniffing cadaver dogs. Investigators came to the site armed to shoot any wild hogs that came near.

"If her body is here," one investigator told Dawn in an ominous tone. "She would be eaten within six hours."

The search was frantic in the beginning but investigators seemed to lose hope after a few days passed. Britt's family returned home to Rochester with sunken hearts.

Brittanee's little brother chastized her friend upon their returning, stating "I thought you were bringing Brittanee back!"

Eight months later, police still had no promising leads. They would get an anonymous tip to check out an area a few miles north of the original search area near the Scantee River.

Once again, they came up with nothing. But a couple out fishing found a pair of sunglasses that looked as if they would belong to a teenage girl.

Neither her parents nor her boyfriend recognized the sunglasses as belonging to Brittanee. A DNA test was performed on the glasses and nothing was found.

Her mother continued to believe that she's alive.

"I think she was taken and held against her well," Dawn said. "I think she has become the victim of human trafficking."

Investigators and reporters shot down the notion, however. Typically, human trafficking occurs where the victim has a language barrier and Myrtle Beach was not exactly a hot bed for that type of crime. The police did not rule it out but it is low on their list of possibilities.

From 1997 to 2010, South Carolina has reported 12 cases of documented sex tracking. All were women, according to Doors to Freedom, an organization that helps victims of sex trafficking.

A few months later, police would receive some cell phone footage of Brittanee shot by a young man she had met. There were a group of teens antagonizing her and she wanted the young man's help to hang out with her so they would stop. He shot some footage of her sitting by herself, texting her boyfriend. He has since been cleared of any suspicion as he did have an alibi.

Pressed for suspects, law enforcement looked at every possible lead.

Three years later, authorities identified fifty-one year old Raymond Moody as a person of interest. They obtained a search warrant for a Georgetown motel room where Moody rented out at the time of Brittanee's disappearance. They noted that Moody had received a traffic ticket in Surfside beach just one day after Brittanee went missing.

Moody was a a registered sex offender, having raped a nine-year old girl in 1983. He was released in June of 2004. But Moody did not cooperate with investigators and remained tight-lipped under interrogation.

He is also a suspect in the case of Crystal Soles who disappeared in January of 2005.

"We've heard his name before," Dawn Drexel said. "It's a possibility the cases are connected. We don't know what happened to Crystal or Brittanee."

Moody lived in an area where Brittanee's cell phone last pinged. He was referred to as "Mr.Clean" because of his resemblance to the bald character in the Mr. Clean commercials. He has not been mentioned in any police reports since 2012, however.

The FBI would get involved and offer their belief that Brittanee was abducted and taken to a "stash house" where she was raped and then murdered. Her body was then wrapped in plastic and she was thrown into an alligator pit where her body would presumably be eaten.

This narrative was offered by FBI Agent Gerrick Munoz who obtained the informaton from an inmate named Taquan Brown. Brown is serving a 25-year sentence for a different case but stated he was present during Britt's last moments.

He said he had seen Britt when he visited a "stash house" which was a moniker used by drug dealers to describe a place where they stashed weapons, money or drugs.

Brown stated that Taylor picked Britt up in Myrtle Beach and took her to McClellanville. Once there he "showed her off, introduced her to some other friend that were there...they ended up tricking her out with some of their friends, offering her to them and getting a human trafficking situation."

The stash house was in the McClellanville area, the last location where Britt's cell phone was pinged.

Brown told the officials that he saw Da'Shaun Taylor, who was 16 years old at the time, and several other men "sexually abusing Brittanee Drexel."

Brown then claimed he went to the backyard to give Da'Shaun's father money.

During this time, Britt tried to escape. She was caught by one of the men who "pistol whipped" her across the head. She was then taken back inside the house.

Brown stated that he heard two gunshots and then saw the woman being wrapped up and removed from the home.

The FBI agent revealed that "several witnesses" have told him that she was dumped in a pond that was filled with alligators.

Taylor has since been convicted of robbery in 2011 and could face a life sentence. He stated that he knows nothing of Britt's case and with the lack of evidence he has not faced any charges in her disappearance.

Chad Drexel, however, thinks Taylor may have been involved.

He recalled a time when he was out handing out Brittanee's missing person fliers and handed it to Taylor who was in his car.

"I gave him the flier," Chad said. "He had a car full of brothers, friends. He handed the flier to one guy in the back seat. They all laughed and then drove away and threw the flier out the window."

"I got mad. I said 'There's something about this guy...'"

After the information was released to the public, Taylor's mother, Reverend Joanne Taylor, immediately defended her son.

She stated that he had already served his time for the robbery (a McDonald's restaurant) and that he was a "great kid" that was only

16 years old at the time of Brittanee's disappearance. During her son's hearing, Taylor's mother took the stand and said the following:

"And I want to say that at the time of this alleged abduction, he was 16 years old. I was never a mother thatwould let my kids run loosely, and definitely not with the father, you know, out to do things. I kept great hold on him. I am a pastor of a church. They were in church, they had a strict bedtime, I knew every place that they went. MyrtleBeach would not be a place that he would go at the age of 16. So I just, you know, I ask for your fairness, I ask for, you know, the correct justice in this case. And know that he is not a flight risk. I mean, I teached them good values, I instill in them what few things that have happened, they have exemplified overall what I've taught them. He is not, you know, a flight risk or anything.

Chad Drexel read the testimony and immediately took to his own Facebook page.

I would like to set the record STRAIGHT with a STRONG REPLY to Joan Taylor's comments to the Post Courier in South Carolina this past Friday.

Based on evidence the FBI and the Myrtle Beach Police department has gathered, along with FACTS and SPECIFIC INFORMATION gathered from a team of Private Investigators that I HIRED to work with local law enforcement actively during the case (which will SOON COME TO LIGHT) – we have no doubt Timothy Da'Shaun Taylor played a significant role in the abduction and murder of my daughter.

Of course the mother of Timothy Da'Shaun Taylor is going to defend her son – as a father I can understand a need to defend your children. What I DON'T understand is defending your children when you must KNOW the truth.

Her assumptions and words stated have been verified INCORRECT and couldn't be farther from the TRUTH. We know Timothy Da'Shaun Taylor was witnessed by others (Witnesses NOT IN JAIL) with my daughter – we are just praying that they do the RIGHT thing and stop forward with what they know. Additionally he has been seen and followed to the EXACT area where my daughter's DNA was found. Joan Taylor claimed that the FBI and government are falsely accusing her son because of witnesses IN JAIL?! Well, we have other specific evidence, that I can NOT disclose at this time for the safety of my daughters case, which corroborates these testimonies!! Timothy Da'Shaun Taylor is KNOWN to be involved in dog fighting, bringing drugs to parties, and raping women (mostly Caucasian young women) he either picks up UNWILLINGLY or friends of friends that end up being drugged and taken there. This IS ONLY THE BEGINNING!! There is a TON more "EVIDENCE and HORRIBLE INFO" we would like the PUBLIC in that area be aware of for their safety, but we are unable to disclose at this time.

WITHOUT A DOUBT ....Timothy Da'Shaun Taylor is a suspect in my daughter's Disappearance and Murder! My family and I will be following the FBI's requests to keep specific details in our daughter's case under wrap until THIS HORRIBLE PIECE OF TRASH goes to Prison for Life. After the guilty verdict, we will be happy to dispel these fairy tales that are being spun by Timothy's family. It is disgraceful the way this FAMILY and their FRIENDS are supporting and claiming innocence of a "PROVEN"

FELON without even looking at the evidence presented and the FACTS surrounding the case.

Also adding this PIECE OF TRASH photo so everyone can see WHO HE IS!

On March 25th, 2017, FBI agents called Dawn Drexel to inform her they may have located Brittanee's remains. They are now searching an area 45 miles north of their previous search spot.

After two days, however, they gave up the search.

The case is ongoing.

MISTY COPSEY

Misty Copsey was fourteen years old when she disappeared on September 17th, 1992 after a trip to the Puyallup Fair.

Her case remains a showcase of administrative screw-ups and dropped balls. She was initially thought of as a runaway before foul play was finally suspected a month after the fact. Subsequently, there have been at least five people suspected of committing her abduction.

But the Puyallup police did not get within sniffing distance of Misty or charging anyone with her disappearance. Three different police chiefs and numerous detectives all took a swing at the case and whiffed. No one in law enforcement has been able to answer the question on everyone's lips.

What happened to Misty Copsey?

A GOOD GIRL

Misty was born in 1978 to Diana and Paul "Buck" Copsey. Her father was a firefighter but the couple split up shortly after she was born and Misty lived with her mother.

Misty got good grades in school, excelling particularly in Math. During her last quarter at Spanaway Lake Junior High School, she got A's and B's. Athletic, she played softball, volleyball, and basketball before breaking both forearms during an athletic practice.

Misty was not the ringleader of a bad crowd. She was diffident but funny, entertaining her friends while skipping around and singing the theme song to Sesame Street.

She did not have much in regards to material wants. Her mother eked out a living as an in-home care nurse and they lived in a mobile home park until she was fourteen. Seeking a better place to live, Diana and Misty moved into a duplex where she now had her own room. But Misty longed for her friend who lived in and around the old trailer park. She would make it back there when she could to just hang out.

Tall, blonde and with green eyes, Misty was cute enough to draw the attention of boys. She remained chaste, however, and was not dating like so many of her other friends.

Her innocent, girl-next-door looks would draw the attention of Rheuban Schmidt. Rheuban looked like a casting call actor for a meth head. He sported a reverse mullet, a hairstyle that was cut close to the sides with curls on top. He had beady, green eyes that screamed low IQ. One of Misty's friends described him as a "scuzzy looking dude" but he nonetheless befriends Misty, much to the chagrin of her mother.

Diana grew suspicious of the relationship as Rheuban was four years older and a high school dropout. On one occasion, she listened in on the other end of a phone conversation Misty was having with Rheuban.

"I get horny just looking at you, Misty," Rheuban said, whispering like an old pervert.

Diana became enraged and ordered her daughter off the phone.

"Don't ever talk to that idiot again...."

ENTER CORY BOBER

Cory Bober was a thorn in the side of police every since the Green River killings became a national news story. He would insist that the police are "incompetent fools" while organizing his own searches for her remains. Diana would later accuse him of killing her daughter but he would respond by telling Diana that she was being "ungrateful." He was, after all, the only man on the case.

Bober was a recluse without a vehicle or a drive's license. An inveterate marijuana user, he had a record for both possession and dealing. He was also obsessed with cases of murdered or slain women in his home state of Washington. He had a stack of binders with autopsy reports, pictures, and other arcane details.

Bober came under the radar of the police in Puyallup when he became obsessed with the Green River Killer case. He had a brief acquaintance with Randall Dean Achziger, remembering a conversation where the man told him that the killer inserted rocks into the remains of his victim. Bober became suspicious as that would turn out to be a piece of information only known to police. He then went on a one-man crusade to prove the guilt of Achziger. Bober would interview his ex-girlfriends, friends, co-workers and present all of this in an affidavit to the courts.

Achziger found it ridiculous and annoying.

So did the police.

The Green River Killer would turn out to be a painter named Gary Leon Ridgway.

Bober didn't give up, however. He knew Achziger was the guy.

Bober had his own theories about who was performing the killings. Some were wild and outlandish conspiracy theories. Others were spot on. He would notice that there were victims that "had disappeared on the very same date that others were discovered. Some victims seemed to almost 'commemorate' the deaths or discoveries of others; one would die on a particular date and another would disappear a year to the day later on the very same date."

The police dismissed his theories as the rantings of a crack head. But Bober would be willing to show the proof of his connect the dots calculations. He pointed to the cases of Kim Delange, a 15-year-old killed in 1988 and Anna Chebetnoy, a 14-year-old killed in 1990. Both of their bodies would be found along Highway 410, east of Enumclaw.

Bober discovered that the remains of both girls were found in the same section of 410. The girls were found two years and one month apart. He felt that the killer was following a pattern.

He called the police department and left a voice mail. He predicted that a teen girl from Puyallup would disappear and her remains would be found on Highway 410 in the same vicinity where the other girl's bodies were found. Bober gave him the name of the man whom he felt was the serial killer.

Randall Achziger.

But the police were now used to his calls and viewed him as a crank. A nutcake with a strange vendetta.

His prediction would be half-right, however.

There would be no body found on Highway 410.

But a teenage girl would disappear.

Her name was Misty Copsey.

A NIGHT AT THE FAIR

On September 17th, 1992, Diana told her daughter Misty and her best friend Trina Bevard to behave themselves. Misty had convinced her mother to let them stay out that night...free of any meddlesome adults. But Trina's guardian would not allow her to go without an adult driving them home.

Diana worked as a caregiver for a 97-year-old Alzheimer patient who could not be left alone. She would not be able to drive the girls home. But Misty checked the bus schedules and convinced her mother that they would be okay. There was a bus that left the fair at 8:40 p.m.

Misty then convinced her mother to lie to Trina's guardian, Marlene Shoemaker.

"No worries," Diana said to Marlene. "I'll bring them home."

She wanted to be the cool parent, different from the stuffy adults who forgot what it was like to be fourteen. If it meant telling a white lie so her little girl could have some happiness, so be it.

What was the worst that could happen?

Diana dropped the girls off and gave them one last warning.

"Get home safe."

It would be the last time she would ever see her daughter again.

THE PHONE CALL

A few hours later, Diana would then receive a phone call from Misty as she tended to her elderly patient. Misty told her that she had missed the bus but could get a ride from Rheuban Schmidt.

Diana, knowing what kind of unsavory character Schmidt was, adamantly refused. She told Misty to find someone else to give her a ride back. Misty had an electronic diary which she used to store phone numbers. She told her mother she would find someone trustworthy to call for a ride.

"You call me back when you find someone," Diana said.

"I will. I promise."

Diana would wait all night for the phone call.

In the ensuing hours, Misty would not call back.

Worried, Diane called home in the hope that Misty had gotten a ride without calling her.

No answer.

Diana didn't panic. She figured that Misty went home with that scumbag Schmidt and didn't want to get yelled out for disobeying her.

She's going to get yelled at either/or. All Diana wanted was for her daughter to be safe.

Her shift finally ended and Diana drove back home in a rush.

Upon entering her house, she called out for Misty.

Silence.

She went into Misty's room and saw that it had been untouched from the previous night.

Diana would call the police in a panic. She told them that her daughter had not come home from the fair. The dispatcher would tell her that the police could not do anything about it for thirty days as it "sounded like a runaway case."

Diana knew otherwise.

Trying to calm herself, she figured that Misty was with Trina, that the two of them would be okay.

She called Trina's home.

No answer.

She then began scorching the earth with phone calls.

She would call Rheuban but he told her that she called but he didn't have the gas to go get her. She then called numerous friends of Misty and her mother.

No one had seen Misty.

She called Trina's home again, got no answer, then drove out to her house. She then went to the police department and filed a formal report with the Pierce County's Sheriff's Department who handled runaways as opposed to the Puyallup Police.

MISTY'S MISSING

Misty's friend Trina called Diana after she came back from school. She told the frantic mother that she didn't know where Misty was.

"The last time I saw her, she was heading for the bus," she said.

Diana would call Rheuban again. She would get his roommate this time, James Tinsley.

Diana needed answers. She interrogated the young fifteen-year-old like a grizzled police detective. She asked if Rheuban had been home all night. James then told her that Rheuban and his uncle went to pick up Misty but that he wasn't home just yet.

Later, Diana would call back and Rheuban would tell her that his roommate got the story wrong. He went to a party instead and didn't pick up Misty. He didn't know where she was.

Diana pleaded for the police to do something. They dragged their heels and began talking to some of Misty's friends. "Just call if she calls," they informed them. "No one gets in trouble."

Diana printed fliers with Misty's picture. She plastered them in and around the fairgrounds while calling the media.

The one woman search team would yield no leads. Rheuban would stop by and ask if the police had found anything yet. Diana would then wait at the bus stop near the fairgrounds to inquire with different drivers on the route. She found one driver who said that he saw Misty. She had asked when the next bus to Spanaway was arriving. The driver said it wasn't and that he was done for the night. He gave her instructions on which bus to take but she walked away before he could complete his sentence.

AN ERROR OF JUDGEMENT

Among the many mistakes that the Puyallup police made in the investigation of Misty's disappearance was to make the assumption that she was a runaway. Why they didn't entertain the prospect that she could have been kidnapped and murdered gave the abductor precious time to cover his tracks.

The police came to this erroneous conclusion after they interviewed Misty's mother, Diana. They thought she was a liar and an alcoholic. They then interviewed a pair of Misty's classmates who really didn't know her that well or accompany her to the fair.

A series of cover-ups then ensued, as the police told the media Misty had been found (where they got that information remains a mystery) and made no further investigation.

Until Diana and the media started to make a fuss. The department had to save face and eventually one of the detectives believed that this was not a runaway case.

Misty's disappearance could not be ignored any longer.

Police would talk to the various fair workers and security guards. No one had recalled seeing Misty.

The police then turned to her family, interviewing and doing background checks on both Misty's father, Buck, and Diana.

Their impressions of the duo would support their initial theory that Misty runaway. Diana was an alcoholic with multiple DUIs and seven years prior she had been convicted of welfare fraud. Buck confirmed that his daughter and Diana would have their issues.

Carver then discovered that Diana had filed a runaway report on Misty a month prior to her disappearing.

Diana would later state that the report was wrong. She thought Misty had disappeared then found her in the bedroom. She was too ashamed to tell the police it had been a false alarm.

With the police questioning and media coverage, Misty Copsey was now the talk of her Spanaway Lake Junior High school.

Rumors would abound at the school, one of which came from Misty Matthews who said that Misty had called her from Olympia. Another student stated that she saw Misty at a Color Me Badd concert at the fair.

The rumors were enough to prompt Carver to remove Misty from the FBI's National Crime Information Center as a missing person. He would once again treat her as a runaway.

BOBER'S THEORY

Cory Bober's knew he was right. He knew that police would find a body of a young woman off Highway 410.

He waited but nothing happened.

Until his mother showed him the flier of Misty's disappearance.

Right again!

Heart racing, he called the number on the flier. Bober would get into contact with Diana and hurriedly told her all about his research.

He talked about the Green River Killer, where and how he killed his victims. He would tell Diana that her disappearance was connected to the same guy responsible for the murdered Puyallup Girls, Kim Delange and Anne Chebetnoy.

Cory would apologize to Diana because he knew that Misty was dead. He predicted her body would be found somewhere along Highway 410.

The two would form an uneasy alliance. Bober became Misty's personal avenger. He would start a phone/letter/media campaign to prove the police wrong and himself right.

Misty was no runaway.

She was a victim of Randall Achziger.

In October, however, Bober would be arrested for selling marijuana. He was then accosted by Sgt.Herm Carver who tired of the young man meddling in police affairs.

"He walked in the room I was being held in – looking tired and pissed off. He said, 'I got out of bed tonight, and came down here to meet you – just to see what kind of a hypocrite you REALLY ARE!'

I said (being cocky), 'It's not MY FAULT – HERM – that you don't believe Misty Copsey's MISSING!!'

He yelled (angry), 'DON'T YOU EVER CALL ME BY MY FIRST NAME – IT'S SGT. CARVER TO YOU!!!'"

Bober's journals, November 1992

THIRTY DAYS MISSING

Sgt. Herm Carver and Deputy Brian Coburn would each individually warn Diana of the troublemaker that Bober was. Still, the worried mother would welcome his assistance as she needed all the help she could get. After numerous phone calls, the two would finally meet after a month of Misty being missing. Diana had nowhere else to turn but to the shaggy-haired twenty-six-year-old who lived with his parents.

The police were going through the motions on their end. Carver reactivated Misty's name on state and national lists but only because he was legally required to do so. At this point, he still believed Misty to be a runaway and doubted Diana's veracity.

Meanwhile, Diana would find Cory Bober's constant badgering to be annoying. It got so bad she filed a restraining order against him.

"My daughter has been missing for six weeks from the Puyallup Fair," Diana wrote in the restraining order. "Cory Bober has called me on a daily basis, telling me my daughter is dead. I was advised by Deputy Brian Coburn to file this complaint if I felt threatened."

The order would only last two weeks. Diana would then call the courts and rescind her request. She would later call Bober and apologize. Her daughter had been missing for over 56 days. Bober was annoying as hell but he was the only one doing research. The only one who cared.

Bober organized a volunteer search for Misty in the Green River area. He somehow coerced someone on the police forensic team to tell him the general vicinity of where one of the Puyallup girl's body was found. Bober surmised that Misty's body would be found in the same general area.

Seventy-two days after Misty had gone missing, there was now a volunteer team searching for her.

Nothing came out of the search.

But Diana would later spot Rheuban at a grocery store and confront him. The young man ran and got into a truck with an older man. She saw the look of fear and apprehension on both men as they sped off.

Diana would then lapse into a depression. She tried to commit suicide with booze and prescription drugs.

The next day she would wake up in a hospital. She would spend the next day there, drying out until being discharged back into the nightmare that had become her life.

A PLEA TO THE PUBLIC

Four months after Misty's disappearance, Diana would appear on a local TV station for a special on the Green River Killer. Jim Doyon, the homicide detective who worked the case, spoke of the killings but deferred on stating if Delange and Chebetnoy(the slain Puyallup girls) were connected.

Doyon took an interest in Misty's case. He would journey to Highway 410 and search near milepost 30 where the bodies of Delange and Chebetnoy had been discovered.

Like Bober and the volunteer search team, he too came up empty.

Bober was undaunted and organized another search. He realized that they had been searching in the wrong spot. They were searching on the south side of the highway when the should have been searching on the north.

Twelve people would show up for the search. Diana would arrive with her older sister, Debra. Bober would arrive with Al Hensley, the father of one of the slain Puyallup girls along with his 14-year old Boy Scout nephew, Jaremy Brown.

It would be the Boy Scout that would make the find

Poking into a ditch with his stick, he saw the crumpled blue jeans. Socks fell out of the jeans.

Baggy and stone-washed, they were cuffed at the bottom. The same jeans that Misty had borrowed from her mother on the night of the fair. The jeans were too big for her and Diana remembered them cuffing them on the bottom.

Bober became excited. He knew that the killer had planted the jeans there as a taunt.

He was right. The police were wrong.

But Diana, according to her sister, "broke into a million pieces."

THE KILLING FIELD

Seven dead women had been found in the nine-mile stretch between Enumclaw and Greenwater in the eight years prior to Misty's disappearance.

The two slain Puyallup girls were found in the same area in 1988 and 1991, only one hundred feet apart. They were left off a footpath that had been hidden by thick brush.

Both of the teenage girls had been presumed abducted from the Puyallup shopping center. Detective Jim Doyon believed privately that the cases were connected. He arrived at the site where Misty's jeans were found and interviewed witnesses, particularly Diana and Bober.

The jeans were taken to the lab and the forensic analysis indicated that the jeans had been in the ditch for some time.

Police suspected that someone (Bober? Diana?) had planted the jeans there.

What was undeniable that the jeans were found only a ten minute walk away from where the bodies of the two slain Puyallup girls were found.

SUSPICIONS ARISE

People began to talk. There were reporters who believed the jeans were planted there. Some were talking as if Diana and Bober were lovers and had plotted this for some insurance money.

Dede Miles, a fifteen-year-old friend of Misty, would come to Sgt. Carver with a tip. She said there was a boy that kept coming over to Misty's parties. He would always leave before her mother came home.

His name was Rheuban Schmidt.

Finally, the unkempt looking young man would come under the radar of the police.

Diana, meanwhile, began to suspect Cory Bober.

How did he know where to look? Why was this stranger so interested in the case to begin with? How did he know so much?

The police had warned her to stay away from him. Now she felt compelled to tell the police of her suspicions.

"Diana comes to station. Now feels Cory Bober may be involved in Misty's disappearance. I asked Diana to submit a written statement to that effect and why she feels he may be involved – she agreed to do so."

Carver's notes

AN INTERVIEW WITH TRINA

Detective Jim Doyon would interview the fifteen-year-old Trina Bevard, the last person to see Misty alive.

Six months had passed. Doyon had brought along the jeans with him, the sight of which made Trina cry.

"It seems to me like something that Misty was wearing that night," Trina said. "It looks very close to what Misty was wearing. The socks, they match what she was wearing. The jeans are big, so – her jeans were baggy that night, that she was wearing. They're – they were light blue like they are in the photo. It just seems, you know, it was the clothes that she was wearing."

Doyon would go on to ask what she was wearing (a pullover) and if she had any jewelry. He then asked if she had any cigarettes or birth control pills.

"No," Trina said. "She was straight. She was a virgin. She didn't smoke, she didn't drink, she didn't do drugs. She was clean, so she had no reason to do anything. She wasn't sexually active."

Trina then revealed that the girls made five calls to Rheuban. They could not get a hold of him. They finally got him on the line and he still refused to pick them up even when the girls offered him money. Misty told him about a key under the front doormat of her home. He could go inside, get money for gas and come pick them up.

Trina stated that she didn't trust Rheuban but only because he didn't keep his word and come pick them up. She then called a 23-year old friend named Mike Rhyner for a ride but they got disconnected. The girls were then stranded. They walked downtown to get to the bus stop before spotting a phone booth by a convenience store. Misty then called her mother, telling her that if Rheuban didn't come pick her up she would take the bus. The two argued as Diana didn't want Misty around Rheuban.

Trina had to get home by 10 p.m. She had about an hour and a half to get home which wasn't that far. Misty could not walk the ten miles to Spanaway.

Trina then decided to walk. She gave Misty her extra money for the bus.

"At that time I made my decision of walking home and she said she would take the bus," Trina recalled. "The last words that I said to her were 'Be careful,' and she turned around and told me the same and we walked off in different directions"

Trina also dismissed the notion of Misty being a runaway.

" Her mom just bought her a stereo and she was so excited and she went shopping and she got new clothes,"Trina recalled. She was telling me all about it. She was really excited about it.

BOBER GOES TO JAIL

Meanwhile, Bober would be sentenced to fourteen months in prison for the marijuana possession. He felt that the sentencing was too punitive and threatened law enforcement that they would never find Misty without him. His fellow inmates thought he was crazy and began calling him "snitch" and "The Green River Killer".

Jail would not slow down Bober's efforts, however. He continued to research and write Misty's mother.

"Dear Diana,

...When we found Misty's clothes, part of me died and I watched a part of you die too (much more than a "part") and I was at a total loss for words. I never wanted to be the one to show you your most horrible fears were true and that your daughter is truly dead at the hands of a sick murderer. I will never rest until the killer (Randy Achziger) is brought to justice and dead, if it takes my life to do it."

AMERICA'S MOST WANTED

Misty's case would eventually be broadcast nationally as it was featured on the America's Most Wanted television show.

Over twenty-eight tips came into Sgt. Carver from people who watched the broadcast.

When the tips went nowhere, Diana's suspicions returned to her original suspect, Rheuban Schmidt. She wanted Carver to speak to the young man but the Sergeant would take a circuitous route to get to Schmidt.

Carver would speak to Frank Rodriguez, the owner of Adam's Ribs, a restaurant where Rheuban worked. He convinced the owner to try and find out how much Rheuban knew about Misty.

"3-4-93 @ 1500: Frank states Rheuban said the following during a lengthy conversation about Misty Copsey:

- Yeah, I know about it.

- I know exactly where she is buried.

- They found the clothes but she is buried 6 miles from there.

- They're off by 6 or 6 1/2 miles."

— Excerpt from Carver's notes

Carver would then wait for Rheuban outside the restaurant before his shift started. Schmidt arrived, saw the cops and immediately ran off. The detectives would eventually catch up with him.

Rheuban would concede that he had received calls from Misty the night of her disappearance. But his story corroborated with Trina's, he told the girls he had no gas and could not pick them up.

Carver then asked if he knew where Misty was buried but Rheuban was adamant that he "said those things to get Frank off my back."

Rheuban then revealed that he suffered from "black outs". He stated that he did not recall anything until the daylight hours of September 18th, 1992.

The detectives pounced, asking if it was possible that he blacked out, picked up Misty and harmed her.

Rheuban claimed he didn't know.

All he knew was that he drove out to his grandmother's farmhouse and couldn't recall why.

Detectives would then give Rheuban a polygraph test.

They would later state that the suspect "zoned out" during the test, nearly falling asleep. The tests were inconclusive but detectives felt as if he were trying to beat the test.

A LITTLE LIE

Rheuban fell off the detective's radar when Carver talked to Dede Miles again. Dede would tell the detective that Trina had not walked home from the fairground like she told him.

Dede said that Trina had a boyfriend come pick her up and didn't want anyone to know.

Trina's boyfriend's name was Michael J. Rhyner. He had nothing on his record aside from traffic stops but he had friends that were connected with Chebetnoy and Delange.

He also had a complaint when he was sixteen years old. He was accused of an abduction rape wherein he used a knife and a cigarette lighter to terrorize an eleven-year-old.

Charges were never filed for an undisclosed reason.

Carver brought Trina in for more questioning. He wanted the truth. The truth about who picked her up that night. The truth about Misty.

But the truth was that Trina told the Sgt. Carver and Detective Tom Matison that she lied because she feared "getting into trouble with her guardian about it."

Trina admitted that she called Rhyner, got disconnected and left a message. She told Misty that they could both ride with Rhyner but Misty said no.

"Trina would not be specific why Misty did not trust Rhyner, but the indication was that Rhyner might have 'come on' to Misty at one time and she did not like it. Trina states that she and Rhyner are friends, but not involved."

— Matison's notes

Trina said that she started to walk and then Rhyner picked her up and dropped her off. The detectives asked if perhaps Rhyner had picked up Misty but she said no.

FRANK RODRIGUEZ' FOLLOW UP

Diana would state that Frank Rodriguez, Rheuban's employer, would call her to say that Rheuban had "bragged about doing something" to Misty with his uncle. Frank didn't fully believe him, however, as Rheuban was "weird" and always bragging about stuff he didn't do.

Diana then approached Carver about Rheuban and the sergeant went ballistic.

"We have our man!" he said.

The man he sought was Michael Rhyner, Trina Bevard's boyfriend.

"We share our knowledge of Mike Rhyner and how he is involved with Misty and Trina – and the fact Trina lied to Doyon. We state that there is an excellent possibility that Rhyner may be linked to Chebetnoy and DeLange. Exchange of information is extremely beneficial."

— Carver's notes

"Sgt. Carver believes that Rhyner dropped Bevard off, returned to the area of the fairgrounds, located Misty Copsey, convinced her to get into his vehicle and drove off with her."

— Doyon's notes

Police set up a sting on Rhyner. The car mechanic was selling his 1981 blue Ford Escort for $200 bucks.

The buyer was an undercover cop.

He watched as Rhyner hurriedly took out trash from the car before the sale. The police then did a forensic examination of the car.

Meanwhile, Rheuban's green Nova was being crushed at a wrecking yard. The Puyallup police didn't care as the tweaker was no longer on their radar. Also, Randy Achziger, Bober's suspect, had been charged and convicted for the rape of a seven-year-old.

INTERROGATING RHYNER

Ideally, Detectives Matison and Sgt. Carver wanted the forensics back from Rhyner's Escort before they spoke to him. But the wait became interminable and they brought him in for questioning without some evidence to back up their suspicions.

Rhyner's story would match that of Trina's. He picked Trina up and went back home. He said that he and Trina were only "good friends" and he had met Misty only four times. Matison then asked Rhyner if he felt Misty was alive and what should happen to the person who harmed her.

Rhyner knew what the detective was getting at. On his own volition, Rhyner told the detectives about his juvenile complaint from years ago. He stated he had been cleared and knew that was why they were looking at him now.

"First thing I thought, you know, well, that's in my file," Rhyner said. "Now you guys are going to think I did it since it's in my file. About Misty, that's the one thing that worried me."

Rhyner then passed a polygraph test.

Grasping at straws, the police then turned their sights back on Rheuban. If only they had impounded his car when they had the chance...

TOO LITTLE TOO LATE

"Rheuban Schmidt's initial interview with Sgt. Carver and I created more questions than answers. He was very vague about what he did that September 17th and finally said that he had a 'blackout' and 'woke up' at his grandmother's property near Enumclaw.

...Schmidt had told Frank Rodriguez that Misty's body was six miles from where the jeans were found. He now claims that he said this just to get Rodriguez "off his back," and was not a true statement.

He was driving a Green Chev Nova at the time but he no longer has the vehicle. It was repossessed.

Schmidt also mentioned that his Grandmother's property is located in King County by Buckley and is over a hundred acres. The property has cows on it. Few people enter onto the property."

— Matison's notes

Tinsley, fifteen years old at the time of Misty's disappearance, told police the Rheuban was his roommate for only a few months. He described Rheuban as a short-tempered guy who had a thirteen-year-old girlfriend. The girlfriend, Tinsley said, got jealous when Rheuban got a call from Misty.

Tinsley stated that Rheuban had left the apartment in a huff then came back between eleven and one at night.

So Rheuban did not "black out" as he told detectives. N

"What do you think might have happened to her?" Matison asked.

"Um, I couldn't, I couldn't say because I have no idea," Tinsley said.

"Well, can you speculate?"

"With Rheuban, this is just that I, this, this is what I say with Rheuban because I, I figure that um that he, he tried to, he tried to um, get with her or something and she said, she said no and he got all pissed and did something, I don't know, that's just a second guess."

"You think Rheuban would be capable of ah, kidnapping and killing somebody?"

"I think he could," Tinsley said.

Detectives would meet with Rheuban again, relaying the information that Tinsley recalled him coming back to the apartment that night.

But Rheuban remained adamant in stating that he didn't remember what he did. The detectives then drove him out to his grandmother's farm which had over 100-acres...100 secluded acres.

Detective Matison would note that Rheuban's grandmother's house six miles north of Buckley. Rheuban told Frank that Misty would be buried six miles away from where her jeans were found which would place it in the close vicinity of his grandmother's farm. They would go to inquire with his grandmother but she was not home.

They did not follow-up with the grandmother .

Even so, Rheuban's story no longer held up. He told Misty that he didn't have any gas. He lived sixteen miles away from the fair.

But then he stated that he had driven to his grandmother's farm in Buckley then returned home.

A sixty-mile round trip.

Detectives would give him another polygraph test which he passed.

"It appears that Rheuban Schmidt was not involved in the disappearance of Misty Copsey. He, however, has no alibi as to his movements during the evening of her disappearance, as well as no memory; he claimed that he had a blackout. He acknowledges that he left the residence of James Tinsley, but does not remember what he did.

Investigation to continue."

— Matison's notes

ONE YEAR ANNIVERSARY

The local media ran a few more stories on Misty's disappearance as the Puyallup Fair started. The forensic test on Rhyner's test finally came through. There was no match

with Misty anywhere.

Now once again grasping at straws, Carver would turn to Diana and her associates. He would interview Diana's parole officer and one of her ex-boyfriends.

Misty's father, Buck, was asked to take a polygraph test. He gave consent and passed.

"I explained to her that missing person investigations, at some point in time, must eliminate the parents of any wrongdoing. Diana agreed to the examination."

— Carver's notes

Diana would pass her polygraph test but Jim Corey, Doyon's colleague, said that Diana's polygraph would prove to be inconclusive and that perhaps she had something to do with planting the jeans at the location on Hwy 410.

Carver had always had his doubts about Diana and felt that she planted the jeans.

But the leads would eventually dry up. After nine years, Misty Copsey's disappearance would turn cold.

No one was ever charged with her disappearance.

THE AFTERMATH

Diana would hand out fliers at the Puyallup Fairgrounds every year. She was doing more than law enforcement and even the media.

Every now and then, a local reporter would run a story about Misty. A few cranks would call in and say that they knew something but it would lead to nowhere. Then that would be it. Everything would run dry.

Detective Jim Doyon felt that she was deceased.

BOBER TO THE RESCUE

Bober was then caught for marijuana possession again but this time, he pressed for an advantage. He would gain the Washington State Patrol crime lab report on Misty's jeans, compiled after their 1993 discovery.

He argued that the lab report was part of his defense....he gambled and won.

Obtaining the prized document, the amateur sleuth went to work. The report stated there was no blood, no semen. But there were hairs, fibers, and three red paint chips. There were also holes in the left leg in the jeans, above the knee.

Bober knew that somehow, someway, Randy Achziger was involved. That he killed Misty.

The forensic details raced through Bober's head...red paint chips...red paint chips...

He knew that Bober had a red Porsche. He knew that the paint chips would match.

But the police had another suspect they didn't tell anyone about.

Robert Leslie Hickey.

Hickey's hunting ground was the Puyallup area where he specialized in abduction rapes.

He also drove a red Camaro.

Puyallup police had him on their list as a possible suspect but he was never questioned nor did they obtain forensic samples from his car.

Thirteen years later, however, they would collect samples from Achziger's old car. The car had been sold and the new owner was open to having forensics performed on it.

The particles would be sent to a crime lab which already had a backlog of over a year.

With nothing else left to do, the police turned once again to Rheuban Schmidt.

"I think it's worth taking another shot at Schmidt, and we're planning on it. He's been clean since 1993 ...

— Excerpt from notes by Lt. Dave McDonald, March 19, 2006

Only Schmidt had not been clean. He had been convicted of second-degree theft in 2000. In early 1996, he was accused of rape by one of Misty's best friends. He had held a pillow over her face to silence her but two weeks after filing the report, the girl back away from her accusation and did not file charges.

"[She] told me that she would be undergoing counseling related to the rape, but that she did not want to undergo any additional stress that may be caused by further investigation or possible prosecution in this matter.

Case cleared exceptional/refused by victim."

— Pierce County sheriff's report, Feb. 6, 1996

Later in 2006, Puyallup police gathered more reports on Rheuban. One was a domestic violence protection order requested by his wife, the mother of his three children.

"Rheuban has previously told her that if she ever had him served with a court order he'd 1) burn her house down with her and her kids in it, and 2) send 'some guys' to kick in her door and take money from her.

(She) said Rheuban told her that they'd get money from her if they had to beat her, rape her and then rob her.

(She) said Rheuban told her that if it came to that she 'wouldn't be breathing' when they were done with her."

— Pierce County Sheriff's report, Nov. 9, 2006

MISSING PAINT CHIPS

Adding more incompetence to the investigation, the red paint chips found on Misty's jeans would turn up "missing." All that remained inside the bag where the chips were marked was a piece of plastic.

The lab technicians now had no way to match the red chips on Misty's jeans to Achziger's red Porsche.

Bober would claim that the red chips did match and the police were now trying to save face. Diana, however, no longer wants anything to do with him.

Bober would state that the police would tell Diana that they had, in fact, tested the red paint found on Misty's clothes against Achziger's Porsche. Bober discovered that the red paint was missing beforehand yet the police would lie to Diana about the test.

The lies and incompetence that began investigation have seemingly ended it as well. The Puyallup police relied far too heavily on polygraph tests to discount suspects where their own accounts (particularly in the case of Schmidt) were shaky at best. They failed to secure possession of Schmidt's Green Nova which may have proven to provide forensic evidence that Misty was in his vehicle.

Twenty-four years have elapsed since Misty's disappearance.

Her case remains unsolved.

RAILROAD KILLER

They called him the 'Railroad Killer.'

Angel Resendiz earned the nickname because of his penchant for committing his crimes near railroads, using the rail cars as his own personal get-away system.

Committing murder after murder, he was able to elude both American and Mexican authorities for over a decade.

EARLY LIFE

A birth certificate found by the FBI listed his date of birth as August 1st, 1960. He was born To Virginia de Maturino in the town of Izucar de Matomoros in the state of Puebla, Mexico. His mother has stated adamantly that the correct spelling of his surname is Recendis not Resendiz although the killer would have over fifty different aliases throughout his lifetime.

Angel had spent his childhood years with relatives and not with his immediate family. According to his mother, he was sexually abused by an uncle and other pedophiles in the town of Puebla. He would spend his youth roaming the streets, robbing, stealing and sniffing glue. Relatives would later testify that Resendiz was routinely beaten as a child, one time being "jumped" by several other youths who beat him so bad that he bled through his ears. Resendiz would leave home for months at a time then suddenly return mumbling about a coming religious apocalypse.

Legal trouble came early for Resendiz as he was caught trying to sneak into the Texas border at the age of sixteen. This would become the first of numerous run-ins with border patrol agents until he finally made it into the United States, making his way to St. Louis and finding work with a manufacturing company under an assumed name. He even registered to vote with his false identification.

In September of 1979, at the age of nineteen, Resendiz was arrested for assault and car theft in Miami. He was tried and sentenced to twenty-years in prison but was released after only six years and sent back to Mexico.

But he wouldn't stay there for long.

Through numerous attempts of trial and error, Resendiz had learned not only to game the system but to enter and exit the United States with minimal detection.

He learn to use the rail-cars...

AN "INVISIBLE" MAN

Resendiz became so skilled at crossing the border without detection that he began charging for his services. He began to make a living as a human smuggler, transporting Mexicans across the border for a fee.

Resendiz soon developed a reputation for his smuggling skills, often being seen as a 'go to' person in his Ciudad Juarez neighborhood called 'Patria.'

He would make weekly crossings over the border, being arrested only intermittently. He would then be deported back into his native land only to ping-pong back and forth.

Finally, Resendiz would serve prison terms for his crimes. He would be arrested in Texas for false identity and citizenship, getting a year and half worth of jail.

Upon release in 1987, he journeyed to New Orleans and was arrested for carrying a concealed weapon. He received another year and half worth of prison time until parole.

He then went back to his old haunts in St. Louis where he tried to defraud Social Security and receive illegal payments. He got caught and served a three year sentence.

Resendiz then decided small-time burglaries were his deal. He once again illegally crossed the border, journeyed to New Mexico and was caught burglarizing a home. He was imprisoned for eighteen months and upon release he broke into a Santa Fe rail yard, being captured yet again.

"They should have called Resendiz the boomerang man," forensic psychologist Frank Lizzo said. "He knew how to play the game and seemingly had no fear of the system. The system never punished him severely enough for him to stop his crimes, let alone stop crossing the border."

After his last recorded deportation, the killings began.

THE KILLING FIELDS

"He probably started killing somewhere in his late 20s," Douglas said. "He may have killed people like himself initially – males, transients...(he) became angry at the population at large. What America represents here is this wealthy country where he keeps getting kicked out...(he) just can't make ends meet. Coupled with these feelings, these inadequacies, fueled by the fact that he's known to take alcohol, take drugs, lowers his inhibitions now to go out and kill."

Angel's list of victims began in 1986. Continuing to bounce in and out of the United States, he shot a homeless woman and left her for dead in an abandoned farm house. He had met the acquaintance of the woman at a homeless shelter and they became friends. They would later take a trip on a motorcycle together when he felt that the woman disrespected him.

Resendiz would then take out his gun and blow her head off.

The woman allegedly had a boyfriend whom Resendiz shot and killed as well. He said that he dumped his body in a creek between San Antonio and Uvalde. This killing has never been verified aside from what Resendiz revealed to the police during his interrogation sessions.

Five years later, Resendiz would kill Michael White because he was a "homosexual." Resendiz would bludgeon White to death with a brick and leave him in front of an abandoned home.

These were seemingly warm-ups for the more brutal crimes to come which would also include rape.

"Sex seemed almost secondary," FBI profiler John Douglas said when apprised of Resendiz's crimes. "(He is) just a bungling crook ...very disorganized."

Douglas would later concede, however, that it was this disorganization that worked in his favor. Like a true drifter, Resendiz' whereabouts became as elusive as a rational thought in his head.

"When he hitches a ride on the freight train, he doesn't necessarily know where the train is going," Douglas said. "But when he gets off, having background as a burglar, he's able to scope out the area, do a little surveillance, make sure he breaks into the right house where there won't be anyone to give him a run for his money. He can enter a home complete with cutting glass and reaching in and undoing the locks."

"He'll look through the windows and see who's occupying it. The guy's only 5 foot-7, very small. In fact...the early weapons were primarily blunt-force trauma weapons, weapons of opportunity found at the scenes. He has to case them out, make sure he can put himself in a win-win situation."

Resendiz would also leave his weapon of choice up to chance. Whatever the home would have, a statue a mantle piece, a butcher knife, that would become the instrument of murder.

FLORIDA KILLINGS

On March 23rd, 1997, Jesse Howell would be found bludgeoned to death beside the railroad tracks in Ocala, Florida. He was nineteen years old.

"When we got there," Sheriff Patty Lumpkin said. "We see what appears to be a young male, in his late teens or early twenties. Blood around the head area. You could tell by looking at him that he was dead. The first thing I do is make sure that we've got our forensics people on the way, on the medical examiners on the way, and all the investigators that we have called out or either there or en route."

"When those types of things happen it might have been someone who had fallen off a train," Lt. Jeff Owens said. "Or someone who could have been struck by a train."

The authorities quickly ruled out an accident, however, as they examined the body.

"It didn't appear to be an accident," Lumpkin said. "Because if he had been hit by the train the trauma would have been much more extreme. I've seen some deaths from trains and the initial impact from the train would have done more harm to the body."

The forensic team did determine that Howell's body looked as if he were the victim of blunt force trauma.

"We did see a baseball type of cap," forensic scientist Michael Dunn said. "It appeared to have blood on the inside surface of he bill. In addition, there was a pair of wire rimmed eye glasses and one of the eye pieces was missing, one of the lenses was out. This didn't look good either. As we moved closer, we saw that the victim had been dragged to that spot using just the blue jean material around the cuff (of his pants)."

Near the body, they found a brass and rubber coupling. This device was used to link one train car to another. It could also be used as a clubbing weapon.

"It had what appeared to be blood on it (the coupling)," Dunn recalled.

Howell still had jewelry on his person. He wore a gold cross necklace, a watch and a small amount of cash in his pocket. The police ruled out robbery as a motive.

The police did not identify Howell's body right off the bat. They did find a money wire receipt where some money had been wired from Illinois to Florida. The name on the receipt was of a woman named "Wendy."

Police tracked the money transfer to its point of origin which was all the way in Woodstock, Illinois.

Coincidentally, the authorities there were investigating the disappearance of Wendy Von Huben.

Wendy was missing alongside her boyfriend, the nineteen year old Jesse Howell.

"They advised me that they were investigating a John Doe," Woodstock Detective Kurt Rosenquest recalled. "Unidentified male."

Rosenquest then followed up with the investigating team in Florida, sending them the fingerprints and pictures of Jesse Howell.

The Ocala police would then positively identify Howell.

Jesse had met Wendy only months earlier. They had secretly planned to marry and went on a road trip with another couple.

The other couple, however, grew tired of Jesse and Wendy's constant bickering. They demanded to be let out of the car and left. Jesse and Wendy continued into Ocala, Florida where they ran out of money.

Wendy would call her parents in Illinois who would then transfer her $200 via Western Union. The couple would collect the $200 but would not return home.

"We checked Greyhounds," Rosenquest said. "Nobody matching their description ordered buses or train tickets back to the Woodstock area."

Tears were shed as Rosenquest informed Howell's parents that their teen son had been murdered. The investigative team then turned their attention to the disappearance of Wendy.

They held out hope because there were issues between her and Jesse, thinking that perhaps she simply ran off to be by herself.

Police scoured the surrounding areas and used helicopters in all directions around the railroad tracks.

They would find nothing. There was no DNA left behind on Jesse Howell's body either.

Papers and fliers with Wendy Von Huben's information was distributed all throughout Florida up through Illinois.

Authorities also began interviewing the transient population that lived along the railroad tracks.

Two and a half months later, however, Wendy's parents would receive a phone call.

"The phone rang," Rosenquest recalled. "Wendy's father answered the phone. The girl was crying. She said 'I'm sorry. I love you.'"

She would tell the father she was two hours away from Woodstock at a gas station. The father asked for the phone number on the pay phone she was calling from and she said that there wasn't any before hanging up.

The police were not certain that the phone call came from Wendy so they immediately headed out to the gas station where they believe the call took place.

Police tracked down the surveillance video of the gas station. On the video, a woman that physically resembled Wendy entered the gas station.

The phone records, however, revealed that the call did not come from the gas station where the surveillance video revealed a woman who allegedly was Wendy. It came from another gas station where there were fliers posted of Wendy.

Someone had played a cruel hoax as Wendy's parents had added their home number to the fliers

ONE-LEGGED BOB AND A CHANCE DISCOVERY

A year went by without any sign of Wendy.

There was some ray of hope, however, as the railroad authorities called the Ocala police and informed them that the received information from a member of one of the homeless camps. They had a man in custody named "One Legged Bob" who was traveling with a girl and may be responsible for the murder of her previous boyfriend.

"'One Legged Bob' was your typical homeless person," Owens said. "Kinda scruffy. Hadn't shaved in a few days. He had a prosthetic leg that helped him get around. For someone who you might consider crippled, he was far from crippled."

Owens would spend the next eight hours interviewing the only lead he had, a one legged homeless man.

After the grueling interrogation, Owens realized that he had the wrong suspect.

By sheer chance, however, Patty Lumpkin heard about someone they dubbed the "Railroad Killer" during a class she was taking at the FBI.

"They called him the Railway Killer," Lumpkin recalled. "The Angel of Death. He was killing people. Leaving them near the railroad or he was killing them at homes or locations that were close to the railroad.

The FBI knew the Railway Killer as Angel Resendiz.

"We knew that Angel Resendiz was a person that rode the rails across the country," FBI Agent Mark Young said. "We were worried where he'd wind up next. So we decided to make him a top ten fugitive. Maybe the millions of eyes of the public would tell us something."

The strategy worked.

"He was one of the most vile, evil persons that I had ever dealt with," Young said. "It was like every time you turn around there's another murder."

Owens and Lumpkin hoped to talk to Resendiz to query him about Jesse Howell's murder and Wendy Von Huben's disappearance.

"The attorneys representing him at the time in Texas stopped us," Owens said. "They wanted to protect their client from talking. Any defense attorney who represents a criminal will generally tell the person to stop talking to law enforcement."

Resendiz was placed on death row and Texas had a fast execution rate. The two detectives worried that they would lose their chance to interview Resendiz and connect him to the crimes in Ocala.

Owens and Lumpkin decided to mail Resendiz a letter, respectfully asking him if they could interview him. The letter was written in a formal manner and even addressed him as "Senor."

To their surprise, Resendiz responded back and granted them an interview regarding his involvement in Jesse's killing and Wendy's disappearance.

During their meeting, Resendiz was quick to admit that he had killed Jesse. The detectives deliberately withheld information about the killing, holding back details that only the killer would know. But when Resendiz described using a brake coupling from one of the trains, they knew they had their killer.

But they needed to find out what happened to Wendy.

In a follow-up letter, they promised him immunity from prosecution if he agreed to talk. It was a moot point by then as he was already on death row but the detectives still needed permission from Wendy's family to go through with the interview.

In order to receive some sense of closure, the family agreed to the immunity.

"When we get to the prison," Lumpkin said. "We see him coming down the hallway. He (Resendiz) has a waist belt on. It's an electric shock belt and he's chained to the belt. He's just a mild-mannered person but remember that a psychopath or a sociopath doesn't have any feeling. I mean he had dead eyes. He had no feeling in that body. He didn't care about anything."

Resendiz would reveal that he was heading south for work when the train stopped and he spotted Jesse getting off the train for a smoke.

"Resendiz told us that he killed Jesse with a piece of the train coupling," Lumpkin said. "And Wendy was asleep on the train when this took place. And then when they went down the road further somehow he talked Wendy into getting off the train."

Resendiz then raped and strangled Wendy to death.

Resendiz drew a map of where had left Wendy's body. He described burying her in a shallow grave near a canopy of trees. Resendiz would remember that she had a book in a back pack and an army style jacket that he used to cover her fresh grave.

Police would return to the site and were able to locate where he buried Wendy's body. Almost three years after the murder, everything the killer described was still there. The book. The jacket.

And Wendy's body.

"When Wendy ran away she had a small engagement ring," Owen said. "And she had a Winnie the Pooh wristwatch."

The detective would bring those items back to Wendy's parents.

KENTUCKY RAILROAD MURDER

In August of 1997, Resendiz would make his way from Ocala, Florida to Lexington, Kentucky. It was there he would stalk two young college students.

Holly Dunn was a 20-year old junior at the University of Kentucky and it was there she met Christopher Maier.

"Chris Maier was my very good friend," Dunn recalled. "He was just the nicest, kindest man. We decided that we wanted to be more than friends then we started dating. We dated for about three months."

"Chris and I were attending a party. We decided that the party wasn't very fun so we went to go talk a walk by the railroad tracks. We sat down and talked for awhile and when we got up to leave a man came out from behind an electrical box. He had a weapon that he used on Chris. It was some sort of ice pick or screw driver. Something sharp. I guess our immediate thought was he's going to rob us. That's when we realize he wants money we start thinking 'okay, well, you could have our credit card, you can have our ATM card, you can have our car.' Then he started tying up Chris' hands behind his back. And then he came over to me and he took off my belt and that's when I started thinking he doesn't want to rob us."

After tying up Holly, Resendiz then pulled Chris by the shirt across the railroad tracks and into a ditch.

Holly would follow on her knees, pleading for him to stop whatever he was about to do.

"Lie down," Resendiz said, his voice soft but menacing.

"Everything is going to be okay," Christopher said to Holly as Resendiz dragged him into the ditch.

"Shut up!" Resendiz commanded as he gagged Christopher with a sock.

Resendiz then walked off into the darkness. The frightened couple did not know what the psychopath had planned.

"Then he comes with this rock," Holly recalled. "There was no warning, he drops this rock on Chris' head. I'm just thinking 'what just happened?' I don't even know what just happened."

"You don't have to worry about him anymore," Resendiz said to Holly as he got on top of her.

"I went into survival mode, I'm thinking, I mean he's gonna kill me. I may as well fight. I'm gonna fight. He unties my feet and climbs on top of me. I start to kick and scream and hit him but he held that knife or ice pick (to my throat) and said 'look how easily I could kill you.' I stopped everything and then he raped me."

"I memorized his face," Dunn said. "I stared at him and memorized, he had a tattoo on his arm, I was thinking if you have any scars I'm gonna remember your scars, I'm gonna remember your face,I'm not gonna forget it because if I live through this I will get you."

Resendiz completed the sexual assault of Dunn before smashing her head with a rock.

"He hit me five or six times in my face," Dunn recalled. "I think I put my hand up and then I turned over and then he hit me five or six times in the back of my head. He hit me hard. He was trying to kill me. I think I laid there and he thought I was dead."

Resendiz did think she was did as he threw the rock down and ran away from the crime scene.

Holly would suffer severe facial trauma but miraculously survived the attack.

"I had a broken jaw," Dunn said. "Broken eye socket and cuts on the back of my head that they had to staple shut and then I had cuts on my face."

She woke up in a Kentucky hospital, surrounded by family members.

"Everyone was told not to talk about Chris to me. I just said 'Chris is dead, isn't he?' And my Dad actually is the one I said that to and he was like 'yes, he died.'"

TEXAS TERROR

Resendiz would travel to Texas via train and in October of 1988 he flopped down in Hughes Springs. He would enter the home of 87-year old Leafie Mason, attacking the woman with an iron and killing her.

Two months later, Resendiz would sneak into the home of Dr. Claudia Benton, a thirty-nine year old medical researcher who lived in a suburb of Houston near the railroad tracks.

Again, it was a case of a home being to close to the train tracks. The train would provide the perfect cover for the sneaky Resendiz as he realized that the sound of the rail-car racing by would allow him to break in homes without being heard.

He applied the same technique with Benton, breaking into her home, raping then killing her.

Police would find the doctor face down on the floor. Her bedroom soaked in blood, ransacked for any valuables.

He head had been covered in a plastic bag while her body had been covered in a blanket.

"It appears that she (Claudia Benton) was sleeping," recalled Ken Macha, former police sergeant. "He was able to get in and picked up a bronze statuette from the mantle in the living room. He was relentless in beating her. The skull fractures themselves would have been enough to kill her. She was then stabbed in the back with a very large butcher knife."

"Resendiz was brutal, sadistic," said former West University police chief Gary Brye.

Fingerprints and DNA evidence would link Resendiz to the crime.

The problem was they could catch the man that Texas Ranger Drew Carter referred to as "a walking, breathing form of evil."

EVADING POLICE

Seven months later, Resendiz would continue to avoid capture. He remained in Texas, riding the rail cars until coming into the town of Weimar. He would break into the home of Pastor Norman "Skip" Sirnic and his wife Karen. Resendiz smashed a jack hammer into both of their heads, killing them instantly. He would then rape the body of Karen postmortem.

"He would watch these places," prosecuting attorney Devin Anderson said. "He would watch them, wait for them to go to sleep, get in their house and he would strike them before they would even wake up. I thought we have got to catch this guy."

The DNA found at the scene of the Sirnic murders would match those left on Benton. The FBI then realized they had a highly mobile serial killer on the loose...someone who could kill in one town then appear in another town miles away and kill again.

Resendiz was also smart. He would constantly alter his appearance. He'd shave his head. Then his mustache. He'd be clean shaven one week. Unkempt the next. He would wear glasses one week. No glasses the next.

Authorities could not get an accurate description of him other than the fact that he was small.

Resendiz was also able to take advantage of the lack of a coordinated computer system that gave law enforcement the ability to cross-check fugitives. After the Sirnic murders, Border Patrol had encountered Resendiz near the El Paso border but did not find him on the wanted list.

They then deported him back to Mexico.

Within 48 hours, Resendiz was back across the border to resume his killing spree.

"Our computers told us that he was nothing of lookout material," said C.G. Almengor, a supervisor at the border."We really wish he had been in the system so we could have caught him."

Resendiz would be deported no less than seventeen times over the course of his rampage. At no point did authorities make the connection because of his changing appearance, use of different aliases and the lack of a connected system to document illegals trying to come across the border.

A PREFERENCE FOR TEXAS

Noemi Dominguez was a graduate of Rice University who had just recently quit her job as an elementary school teacher to pursue a master's degree.

She was described as "the sweetest, nicest teacher – a darling who went the extra mile."

Fueled by hate, Resendiz would break into Noemi's home and rape her before killing her with a pick ax. He then stole her car and drove to Schulenberg, Texas where he would kill Josephine Konvicka with the same pick ax.

He would leave the weapon embedded in Konvicka's head as well as leave his fingerprints all over the home. He was more than just sloppy, he was getting cocky. He left a newspaper article that described his crimes as well as a toy train...a reference to his nickname as the "Railroad Killer."

Resendiz was also meticulous in approaching his victims.

"He undid the light in her (Noemi's) car," Anderson said. "So when he opened the door it wouldn't come on. That's who were were dealing with. Someone who really knew how to sneak around. Who really knew how to avoid detection."

"He kept killing people. He would not stop. In his mode of transportation, using the railroads was brilliant because they couldn't be monitored. I mean there's thousands of trains and millions of miles of tracks all over the United States."

"I felt hopeless at the time. Because if you're willing to sleep in a train or you're willing to sleep in a field, you can stay lost for a long, long time and I didn't think we were ever going to catch him."

Later that month, Resendiz had journeyed to Illinois, reaching the town of Gorham. He would break into the home of 80-year old George Morber and his daughter Carolyn Frederick. Resendiz would tie Morber to a chair and shoot him in the back of the head with a shotgun. He then raped Carolyn and smashed the shotgun across her head with such force that the weapon broke in half.

Both Morber and Frederick would die from their injuries.

The FBI placed him on their Top Ten list.

They then recruited his common-law wife, Julietta Reyes, and brought her into Houston for questioning from her hometown of Rodeo, Mexico.

Reyes complied with police requests, turning over over ninety-three pieces of jewelry that her husband had mailed to her from the U.S.

Relatives of Noemi Dominguez claimed thirteen pieces. George Benton was able to identify some pieces of jewelry as belonging to his wife as well.

Police would then locate Resendiz's half-sister, Manuela Karkiewicz, who lived in New Mexico. Initially, she refused to cooperate. She worried that the FBI or the police would kill her brother. But Carter convinced her to talk Resendiz into giving himself up.

The FBI knew that Resendiz had made his way back to Mexico after the murders in Illinois and was hiding in his hometown neighborhood of Patria.

Carter was able to get a rapport with Manuela. He convinced her that Resendiz would receive "personal safety while in jail, regular visiting rights for his family and a psychological evaluation."

"I came away with the impression that they (Resendiz' family) definitely had an understanding of right and wrong ... and knew now that what Maturino Resendiz was accused of doing was heinous and wrong ... ," Carter said. "Manuela, especially, came across as a woman of strong faith. There was a very deep emotional strain and burden placed on her in this investigation. She had to make some very difficult choices that impacted her and her family. And, in the end, her actions alone speak to her character."

Carter spent weeks talking to Manuela who in turn "worked a miracle."

They got the serial killer to surrender.

On July 12th, Manuela would receive a fax from the district attorney's office in Harris County which formalized everything that Texas Ranger Carter had promised.

The word passed from Manuela to another relative who acted as a go-between with Resendiz. The relative than came back later that evening and said that Resendiz would surrender in the morning at 9 a.m.

Texas Ranger Drew Carter would accompany Manuela and a spiritual adviser to meet with Resendiz on a bridge that connected El Paso, Texas to Ciudad Juarez.

"When I saw that face there was a little bit of excitement there because I finally said, 'This is going to happen,'" Carter recalled as he remembered Resendiz appearing on the bridge with his dirty jeans, muddy boots and blank facial expression. "He stuck out his hand, I stuck out my hand, and we shook hands."

Resendiz would then surrender to the Texas Ranger.

DEATH PENALTY

Resendiz' attorneys knew that their only hope would be an insanity defense. The Mexican government also got involved, lobbying authorities to spare Resendiz the death penalty

"Insanity was the logical defense because no one wants to believe that there is someone out there who would do things like that," Anderson said. "That was the thing that worried me the most about the case was that jurors would just throw up their hands and say nobody in their right mind could do what he does."

"The thing about what a life sentence with Resendiz would have been, he would have enjoyed it. I mean he would have had pen pals. He would have given interviews if they let him, I mean he would have loved it. And I knew that. And he didn't deserve to live after what he did just didn't. He caused so much pain, so much heartache and so much terror, that's what the whole focus of the trial had to be."

George Benton, the husband of Claudia, would vehemently criticize the Mexican government who support his appeals and domestic opposition to the death penalty.

"(He)looked like a man and walked like a man. But what lived within that skin was not a human being."

"He was small," Anderson said when she first saw Resendiz in the courtroom. "Maybe five- foot five. His forearms though, were roped with muscles. He was scary. Even though he was small you could feel he was dangerous. He looked like a wild animal who'd been caught."

Resendiz looked "timid" in the courtroom and spoke of himself in religious riddles. He claimed he was Jewish and didn't seem effected when he was informed that the prosecution was aiming for the death penalty.

"I don't believe in death," Resendiz, said. "I know the body is going to go to waste. But me, as a person, I'm eternal. I'm going to be alive forever."

The defense said that Resendiz' crimes were caused by head injuries, drug abuse and a family history of mental illness. He has a delusional perception of the world as he believes that he can cause earthquakes, floods, and explosions and that God told him to kill his victims whom they believed to be evil.

He made a living stealing things from his victims and having his wife sell them in Mexico. "That was his job," Anderson said. "And for recreation it was killing the people who lived in the house."

"He was a very intelligent person who worked the system and knew exactly what kinds of things to say to get that defense to work."

The jury, however, would find Resendiz guilty after one hour and forty-five minutes of deliberation.

He was sentenced to die via lethal injection.

"He made it very clear during my conversation with him that he deserves to die," Owens said.

"I want to ask if it is in your heart to forgive me," Resendiz said in his final words. "You don't have to. I know I allowed the devil to rule my life. I just ask you to forgive me and ask the Lord to forgive me for allowing the devil to deceive me. I thank God for having patience with me. I don't deserve to cause you pain. You did not deserve this. I deserve what I am getting."

Resendiz then prayed in Hebrew and Spanish before drawing his final breath.

MISSING MADELEINE

MARY CHILDRESS

Madeleine McCann, a young child of three years old, was visiting the popular Portuguese resort town of Praia da Luiz along with her parents and younger siblings, as well as a group of her parents' close friends, when she went missing on the night of May 3rd. Madeleine's disappearance became an international sensation and various police departments in both Portugal and the United Kingdom, as well as Madeleine's parents, would conduct independent investigations into her disappearance and the circumstances surrounding that night.

Background

Madeleine Beth McCann was born on May 12th, 2003 to Gerry and Kate McCann in the small town of Leicester, in the United Kingdom, before moving to Rothley in Leicestershire as a young child. Both Gerry and Kate McCann were both practicing physicians and prominent members of the local Roman Catholic community, and had a total of three young children at the time of Madeleine's disappearance, Madeleine as well as two younger siblings: a twin boy and girl.

The entire McCann family set out for the popular Portuguese resort town of Praia da Luz (referred to as "little Britain" because of the large amount of British vacationers who frequented the town) on Saturday, April 28th for a family vacation with seven other adults and five additional children.

The McCanns rented a small apartment owned by a retired British schoolteacher through a private vacation company. The unit, a two-bedroom ground level apartment in the resort's Waterside Village, was next door to several of their friends' rented apartments. The unit was accessible from two locations: a sliding glass patio door and a front door facing the popular Ocean Club. The room's sliding glass door and patio overlooked the Ocean Club's facilities, including the tapas bar that Madeleine's parents would dine at the night of her disappearance.

The nine adults who made up the party included the McCann parents, Russell O'Brien, Matthew Oldfield and his spouse, Rachael

Oldfield, Dianne Webster, David Payne, Fiona Payne, and Jane Tanner and her significant other. These friends would later be referred to as the "Tapas Seven," after the tapas bar that they were dining at the night of Madeleine's disappearance.

Night of Disappearance

During the daytime on May 3rd, the group's last night at the resort, the children spent the morning playing at the resort's Kids' Club, also eating lunch with their parents and spending a couple of hours at the children's pool. The last known photo of Madeleine was taken that afternoon by Kate McCann, showing the young girl sitting by the pool next to her father and sister.

On the night of Madeleine's disappearance, her mother put Madeleine and her siblings down for bed around 7:00pm, wearing her favorite Marks and Spencer's Eeyore pajamas. At 8:30pm, the group of nine adults decided to have dinner and drinks at the nearby tapas bar, located just 160 feet away from the hotel rooms that the children were staying in. Kate McCann described the tapas bar as being located directly across the pool from the children's room and being just a 30-second walk away.

The group of adults had requested a table on the patio which overlooked their children's rooms, so that the parents could have peace of mind while dining. Kate McCann has stated that a resort staff member left a note in the message book in the swimming pool area stating that the group of adults was requesting a specific table so that they would have a view of the hotel rooms in which their children were staying in. She has indicated that she believes the kidnapper saw this note earlier in the day and decided to kidnap her Madeleine upon realizing that the children were to be left unguarded at night.

The McCanns stated that the group of adults agreed to check on the children every 30 minutes, with each adult taking a different shift and helping to check on the eight children located in several different rooms. Because the McCann's patio doors could only be unlocked from the inside, the McCanns left the curtain down and doors closed, but left the patio door unlocked. This is presumably how the kidnapper was able to enter the room. It should be noted that the parents also set up a child-safety gate at both the top of the patio stairs and at the bottom, making it extremely unlikely that Madeleine wandered out of the room.

Gerry McCann performed the first check on his children at 9:05pm, and he reported the children as sleeping safely and soundly. However, he did notice that the children's bedroom door, which he had left open just an inch or two, was nearly wide open when he performed his check on the children. This was the last time that either of the parents would see Madeleine.

Matthew Oldfield, a friend of the McCanns and member of the Tapas Seven, volunteers to check on all of the children at 9:30pm (his children were sleeping in the room next door). When he enters the McCann's room, he notices that the children's bedroom door was wide open. However, he states that upon hearing no noises, he left the apartment without physically looking inside of the children's room. He later states that he did not notice whether there was a draft or whether the bedroom window was open. The fact that he volunteered to check on the children and his claim that he did not actually look in the room caused him to be viewed as a primary suspect by the local police department.

Roughly thirty minutes later, at 10:00pm, Kate McCann walks back to her hotel room to check on her children. Kate stated that she entered the apartment through the patio door and immediately noticed that the children's bedroom door was completely open. Noticing nothing amiss and hearing no noises, Kate attempted to close the bedroom door without looking inside. However, the door closed rapidly and loudly, as if there was a strong draft pulling the door closed.

When Kate reopened the door to see where the draft was coming from, she noticed that the children's window and shutter were both open and that Madeleine was missing from her bed. The young girl's blanket and favorite stuffed toy were still lying on the bed, but her daughter was nowhere to be seen. After frantically searching the apartment for Madeleine, Kate began running back towards the restaurant screaming that her daughter had been taken.

Upon hearing from Kate, Gerry McCann asked Matthew Oldfield to go to the hotel lobby and contact the police. The hotel staff called the local police department at 10:30am and began mobilizing their staff and willing guests to help in the search for young Madeleine. The combined 60 hotel staff members and guests searched for Madeleine until 4:30am, screaming her name throughout the resort.

Police Arrival

At approximately 11:10pm, two officers from the national military police arrive to investigate the missing child report. After conducting a brief search of the resort, they contact the local police force to assist with the search. Two officers from the local police force arrive at 11:20pm to begin assisting with the search and to investigate the hotel room. Later that morning, both patrol dogs and search and rescue dogs were brought in to assist with the search for Madeleine. A road block was not put into place until 10:00am that morning.

The initial police response consisted of a variety of mistakes and oversights that prevented crucial evidence from being gathered. First of all, more than twenty different people were allowed to enter the apartment before it was closed off for investigation, potentially corrupting a wide range of evidence. In addition, although police officers did place "Do Not Enter" crime scene tape over the doorway to the children's room at 3:00am, they did not secure the apartment itself from people entering it. In addition, although police did not allow tourists to stay in the apartment for a full month after Madeleine's disappearance, tourists were again allowed to stay in the apartment for several months until it was closed off to the public again in August 2007 for additional forensic testing and analysis.

Police officers also allowed a fairly substantial crowd of people to congregate on the patio, directly outside of the children's window. It is thought that a great deal of forensic evidence was corrupted as a result of this. Additionally, the officer responsible for dusting the children's window and gathering fingerprint evidence did so without using gloves, possibly corrupting yet another set of evidence.

Furthermore, during the manhunt for Madeleine, several additional mistakes were made. The police did not provide a description of Madeleine or pictures of the young girl to the border police or coast guard force until several hours after her disappearance. Roadblocks were also not put into place until 10:00am that morning, meaning that Madeleine could have been in another country by the time key law enforcement figures even began to search for her. Lastly, Interpol, the global anti-crime organization, did not issue an alert about her disappearance for a full five days after she was reported as missing, allowing her kidnappers crucial time to escape and transport her out of the country or even out of the continent.

Child Sightings

Jane Tanner

Jane Tanner, one of the "Tapas Seven," reported seeing a man carrying a child through the resort complex the night of the disappearance. Jane left the tapas bar at 9:00pm to personally check on her own children in their nearby hotel room and reported passing Madeleine's father, on his way back from checking on his own children, during her walk to the hotel room.

While Jane claimed to have seen Gerry McCann on her way to check on her own children, both Gerry and an English vacationer that he stopped to chat with, do not remember seeing her pass by on the very narrow street. This discrepancy later cast doubt on her story and led to Portuguese authorities accusing her of inventing the story.

At approximately 9:10pm, Jane reported that she saw a man and a child cross the street at *Rua Dr Francisco Gentil Martins* and *Rua Dr Agostinho da Silva* heading away from the Ocean Club, towards the east. She described the man looking like a local and as carrying a barefoot child across the intersection. The man was described as being of Mediterranean appearance, dark-haired, roughly 5' 7" tall, and wearing khakis with a dark jacket. The child was seen wearing light-colored pink pajamas with floral patterns. Although Jane reported this sighting to the local police department soon after Madeleine was discovered missing, the police did not release any information on this possible suspect until some three weeks later, on May 25th.

Despite Jane's seemingly important sighting, a later investigation by Scotland Yard would rule out this individual as a suspect. British police were able to identify the man as a vacationer staying in the same resort as the McCanns. He was carrying his daughter back to their hotel room after picking her up from a play hour for children at the resort. It would later be confirmed that his daughter was wearing light-pink pajamas with floral prints that night.

Martin and Mary Smith

Two other vacationers staying at the resort reporting seeing a man carrying a young child the night of Madeleine's disappearance. Martin and Mary Smith reported seeing a man walking down Rua da Escola Primaria, towards Rua 25 de Abril and away from the resort, at approximately 10:00pm that night. The man was sighted just 500 yards from the McCann's apartment.

The Smiths stated that the man did not look like a tourist and that he did not seem comfortable interacting with the child in his arms. The man was described as being in his mid-30s, approximately 5' 8", with short brown hair and khakis on. The child was described as being three or four years old, with blond hair and light colored pajamas. The young girl was also barefoot.

Those Present at Time of Disappearance

The McCanns were accompanied by a group of seven adults and five children on their vacation to Praia da Luz. All seven adults were present at the tapas bar for at least part of the night. Jane Tanner, an English marketing executive, and her partner Russell O'Brien were staying in one room with their two children. Fiona and David Payne, as well as Fiona's mother, Dianne Webster, and their two children were staying in another room. Lastly, Matthew Oldfield and his wife, Rachael Oldfield, were staying in the last room along with their young daughter.

Timeline

7:00pm - Gerry and Kate McCann put their three children to bed. The children are all sleeping in the bedroom closest to the front door.

8:30pm - Gerry and Kate McCann leave the hotel to meet their friends at the resort's tapas bar, located just 160 feet from the hotel room and in sight of the patio door. The parents reportedly leave the patio door unlocked, but the door closed and the curtains drawn.

9:05pm - Gerry McCann checks on the children in their room. He reports that the children were sleeping safe and sound. He stops to speak with another tourist for a few minutes on his was back to the tapas bar.

9:10pm - Jane Tanner recalls seeing Gerry speaking with the English tourist on the street leading back to the tapas bar. Neither man recalls seeing Jane Tanner, which casts doubt on her story given how narrow the street was. Tanner notices a man crossing the street with a child in his arms. This sighting is later ruled out by Scotland Yard detectives.

9:30pm - Matthew Oldfield, a member of the Tapas Seven, visits the McCann's room to check on the children. He notices that the bedroom door is wide open, but upon hearing no noise, he does not go far enough into the apartment to see whether Madeleine is in bed. He does not recall the bedroom window being open at this time.

10:00pm - Martin and Mary Smith, two tourists staying in the same resort, recall seeing a man carrying a barefoot child down the street, away from the resort.

10:00pm - Kate McCann visits the hotel room to check on her children. She entered the apartment through the patio doors and noticed that the bedroom door was wide open and then sees that the window is open as well. She notices that Madeleine is missing and, after performing a quick check of the entire apartment, runs back to the restaurant screaming that her daughter is missing.

10:10pm - Gerry McCann asks the resort to call the police and report Madeleine as missing.

10:30pm - The hotel begins treating Madeleine's disappearance as a missing childrens case. The hotel mobilizes sixty staff members and guests to search the entire resort complex for Madeleine. Reportedly, guests could hear Madeleine's name being screamed out until 4:30am that morning.

11:10pm - Two officers from the Guarda Nacional Republicana, essentially the country's military police, arrive at the resort to conduct a search for Madeleine. After conducting a quick search, they contact the local criminal police department for assistance.

11:20pm - Two officers from the Policia Judiciaria, the local police department, arrive to assist with the search and investigate the McCann's hotel room for clues.

2:00am - Two patrol dogs arrive at the resort to assist with the search for Madeleine.

8:00am - Four search and rescue dogs arrive at the resort to search for Madeleine. Local police officers are called in from vacation and during their days off to assist with the search. They begin searching local waterways, wells, and sewers.

10:00am - Police setup road blocks to prevent the abductor from leaving with the child. The local police department did not ask for photos of cars seen leaving the area at the time of Madeleine's disappearance.

Portuguese Investigation

Portuguese investigators interviewed several witnesses who reported seeing a group of two strange men in the area of the McCann's apartment the morning of the abduction, as well as several days earlier. On the day of Madeleine's disappearance, two men were spotted visiting the area surrounding the McCann's apartment, with one man being spotted on the actual street. The two men, who were visiting the area from 3:30 to 5:30pm the evening of Madeleine's disappearance, said that they were visiting tourist rooms in order to collect donations for a local orphanage. Investigators from Scotland Yard would later say that they believed the two men were casing the street and planning their abduction.

Witnesses would also report seeing several blond-haired men around the McCann's apartment in the days leading up to Madeleine's disappearance. Earlier in the day on May 3rd, a man was seen walking through a gate near their apartment, attempting to close the gate door quietly and without being noticed. Later that evening, at least one blond man was seen standing near the McCann's room at 4:00pm and again at 6:00pm.

At 11:00pm that night, two blond men were seen speaking to each other in loud voices, but reportedly lowered their voices and hurried off upon noticing that they were being observed. Witnesses also reported seeing a man leaning against a wall next to the McCann's apartment the day before the disappearance, with a white unmarked van parked next to the apartment. All in all, several witnesses report seeing suspicious men near the McCann's apartment in the days leading up to Madeleine's disappearance, and report seeing the men staring at or watching the McCann's apartment.

Parents' Reaction

In May 2007, Gerry and Kate McCann set up a private fund to investigate the disappearance of their daughter, calling the organization *Madeleine's Fund: Leaving No Stone Unturned*. Over $2.6 million was raised to help in the search for their daughter, and the British publication *News of the World* offered a $1.5 million reward for information leading to her return or conclusively proving her fate. Despite the creation of the fund, the McCanns were accused of using the money to pay for their mortgage payment on at least two occasions. The fund has yet to make any progress on ascertaining the fate of Madeleine McCann.

Scotland Yard Investigation

In May 2011, Scotland Yard launched its own investigation of Madeleine's disappearance, assigning a team of 29 police officers to the case, along with eight civilian consultants. Scotland Yard investigators eventually settled on the theory that Madeleine had been taken during a burglary gone wrong. Because there had been a rapid increase in the volume of burglaries in that area in the months preceding Madeleine's disappearance (including cases where the burglars had robbed houses on the McCann's block by entering through the window), they theorized that burglars had kidnapped Madeleine after she woke up and saw their faces during the middle of their robbery attempt.

The British investigators also questioned a group of manual laborers who were working out of a white van in that area at the time of Madeleine's disappearance, as well as two convicted child molesters who were reportedly in that general area during that timeframe. However, despite the developments of new leads in the case, British investigators were never able to determine who actually kidnapped Madeleine.

Suspects

Robert Murat

The first suspect identified by Portuguese police was Robert Murat, a British-Portuguese consultant who lived with his mother just 150 yards away from the location where Jane Tanner spotted a man carrying a barefoot child. Three separate members of the McCann's party later stated that they saw Murat near the resort of the evening of May 3rd, although both Murat and his mother told police that he was at home all-evening long.

Police conducted a thorough investigation of Robert Murat and his possessions, going so far as to conduct a forensic analysis on his computer, phone, and video camera, and even searching his home and property with police sniffer dogs and ground-penetrating radar. Despite the police investigation of Murat and his property, he was cleared on July 21, 2008, when the Portuguese justice department closed the case. However, he was questioned again in 2014 by Portuguese police on behalf of Scotland Yard once the case was re-opened.

Gerry and Kate McCann

While Madeleine's parents were initially viewed with sympathy by the media and general public, they soon became suspects in the case. On June 6th, 2007, a German journalist asked the McCanns if they were involved in the daughter's disappearance during a public press conference. Later that month, local Portuguese paper began writing a series of accusatory articles about the McCanns and their role in their daughter's disappearance.

One of the factors that led to so much speculation about the McCanns and their potential role in their daughter's disappearance was the fact that their initial interview with local police was conducted using a translator. The police investigators would ask a question in Portuguese and then have the translator ask the question in English. The McCanns and their friends would then answer the question in English, which was then translated into Portuguese for the police. Finally, the police then typed up the statement provided by the McCanns and members of the Tapas Seven in Portuguese, before verbally reading the statement back to them in English and asking them to sign the document. This constant translation may have contributed to the discrepancies contained in the statements of all those present that night.

There were several inconsistencies in the McCann's statements. For instance, both parents initially said that they entered the apartment through the locked front door when the checked on their children. However, they would later state that they entered the patio doors at the back of the apartment. In addition, the parents alternatively stated that the patio door was both locked and unlocked that night, casting doubt on their statements. Gerry McCann later told a British newspaper that they had used the front door to check on their children earlier in the vacation, but that they started using the patio door because the front door was next to the children's room and woke them up on their bi-hourly check-ins.

The McCanns also provided contradictory statements on the room's exterior shutter. While Kate McCann told police that the shutter was closed when she put the children to bed at 7:00pm, she claimed that the shutter and window were both open when she discovered that Madeleine was missing. Gerry McCann told police that he closed the shutter after discovering that Madeleine was gone. He also said that, after investigating the shutter from outside the apartment, he noticed that it could be opened from outside. However, the local police said that the shutter was incapable of being opened from the outside and that the lack of evidence of forceful entry ruled out the theory that the abductors had entered through the window.

This important detail led the local Policia Judiciaria to concluded that Madeleine had never been abducted and that the McCanns had made up the story to hide some wrongdoing committed by the parents, even theorizing that Madeleine had actually died in an accident and that the McCann had created the abduction story to shield themselves from scrutiny.

After suspicions about Gerry and Kate were made public, two police sniffing dogs were brought in by Mark Harrison, a national search specialist for the British National Policing Improvement Agency, to conduct an investigation of the apartment, as well as items left by the McCanns and their rental car at the time of Madeleine's disappearance. The two dogs were taken throughout the entire resort, including inside of the McCann's apartment; the dogs alerted their handlers that they smelled signs of Madeleine at the apartment, but did not alert their handlers anywhere else in the resort.

Additionally, the dogs also alerted their handlers of a clue directly behind the couch in the apartment, as well as under the veranda of the bedroom that Gerry and Kate were sleeping in at the time of Madeleine's disappearance. Furthermore, upon additional investigation the cadaver dog alerted its handler when walked around the McCann's rental car, particularly around the outside of the car and inside the trunk of the car. However, the Sunday Times would later say that footage of this investigation clearly showed the dog's handler manipulating the dog and encouraging it to signal a find when passing by those locations.

DNA Analysis

On August 8th, 2007, DNA samples from the McCann's rental car were sent to the Forensic Science Service in Birmingham, England, for testing. The low copy number DNA analysis, which is known for its lack of accuracy and inability to draw conclusive results, demonstrated that 15 out of 19 of Madeleine's DNA pieces were found in areas where the cadaver dogs had signified Madeleine had been, both in the apartment and in the McCann's rental car.

Once Portuguese authorities were notified of the results of this DNA test, they officially abandoned the abduction hypothesis and marked Madeleine's parents as official suspects in the case. They even offered the McCanns a plea deal: they would receive a two-year sentence or less if they admitted that Madeleine had died in an accident and that Kate had hidden the body out of fear of being arrested. Gerry McCann cooperated fully with the police and answered all of their questions; however, Kate refused to answer the authority's question on advice from her attorney.

On September 10th, 2007, the head of the local police department signed a report which concluded that Madeleine had died accidentally in the McCann's apartment and that the McCanns had faked an abduction in order to hide their role in their daughter's death.

Conclusion

Despite the views of the Portuguese investigators, as well as the information uncovered by Scotland Yard, it is likely that the truth surrounding Madeleine's disappearance may never be fully known. While the McCanns and members of the Tapas Seven were accused of being involved in Madeleine's disappearance several times over the years, they have repeatedly denied any involvement in the abduction. Furthermore, both the McCanns and several members of the Tapas Seven have won libel suits against news organizations who accused them of being involved in Madeleine's disappearance.

BEAUMONT CHILDREN

It was a warm summer morning on January 26, 1966, when the three Beaumont children left their suburban home to celebrate Australia Day at the beach. The children regularly made the trip by themselves, so their mother felt at ease providing them with bus fare and sending them on their way while she visited and had lunch with a close friend. However, she would return home that afternoon to find that the children still had not returned. That morning would end up being the last time she saw her three children.

Jane (aged 9), Arnna (aged 7), and Grant (aged 4), lived in Somerton Park, a quiet suburb minutes away from Adelaide, South Australia. Their father, Jim Beaumont, was a linen goods salesman who frequently traveled for work and their mother, Nancy Beaumont, was a stay-at-home mother.

The oldest child, Jane, was viewed by her parents as responsible enough to supervise the other children for short trips and adventures, a style of parenting that was the norm in Australia at that time. The children frequently took the five-minute bus ride to neighboring Glenely Beach by themselves and were looking forward to celebrating the national holiday at the beach.

The children left their home at 10:00am that morning and were seen arriving at the beach by witnesses at 10:15am. They spent much of that morning at play on the beach and were supposed to arrive home at 2:00pm. When they did not arrive at the appointed time, their mother assumed that they had become preoccupied with celebrating the holiday with their playmates and that they would arrive on the next bus or had decided to walk home, something that the three children had done before. When the children did not disembark from the next scheduled bus, their mother began to grow worried.

The disappearance of the Beaumont children would result in one of the largest manhunts and police investigations in Australian history.

Furthermore, the event had widespread consequences on Australian society, shattering the illusion that many parents had regarding their children's safety and changing the way that Australians parented their children forever.

Timeline of Events

10:00am - The children leave their Somerton Park home to travel to Glenely Beach by bus.

10:15am - They are seen exiting the bus by multiple witnesses.

11:00am - The three children are spotted playing beneath a sprinkler by an elderly woman. A tall blond man is spotted lying on the ground next to them, watching the children play.

11:15am - A tall blond man is seen playing with the children. They all appear to be laughing and at ease.

11:45am - The children purchase several pastries and a meat pie from the beach snack shop.

12:15pm - The tall blond man and the children are seen leaving the beach together. The children are witnessed laughing together and holding hands.

3:00pm - A postman on his route spots the children walking along Jetty Road alone, away from the beach. The postman is known to the children and they exchange greetings. Police believe that the timeline for this event is incorrect.

7:20pm - The parents of the children become gravely concerned and file a missing children's report with the local police department. Jim Beaumont and the local police search the entire Glenely Beach area.

8:40pm - Police search the surrounding beaches with no results. The father contacts friends and relatives in an attempt to locate the children.

10:00pm - Police issue public radio announcements with a missing children report.

Points of Interest

There are several details in this story which raised doubts with both the parents of the children and the local police department. When the children departed for Glenely Beach in the morning of January 26th, they left with only enough money to cover their bus fare: six shilling and a sixpence. However, the shop owner, who sold several pastries and a meat pie to the children at 11:45am, reported that the children paid for the food with a $1 bill, an amount of money that they did not have when they left their mother's care.

In addition, the shop owner knew the children well and had sold them food and pastries several times before. He reported that the children had never purchased a meat pie before. This suggests that the children received the money from someone after leaving their parents home and that they may have been purchasing the meat pie for someone else.

Lastly, the mother of the children, Nancy Beaumont, repeatedly said that her children were quite shy and very unlikely to speak with strangers, indicating that they may have met the tall blond man prior to the date of their disappearance. Their mother also remembered a seemingly innocuous comment from Arnna, who had previously told her mother that Jane had "got a boyfriend down the beach." Nancy assumed that her daughter was referring to a young playmate, but in hindsight it seems that she may have been referring to the tall blond man spotted by witnesses.

Police Investigation

The South Australian police force began investigating the disappearance of the children in full-force the evening of their disappearance. After interviewing several witnesses who were present at Glenely Beach, they were able to determine that the children were playing with a tall blond, "thin-faced" man while at the beach. He was described as being a blond man in his late 30s with a thin or athletic build.

"Things seemed bungled from the get-go," forensic psychologist Paula Orange said. "First off, the artist drawing the picture admitted to being drunk at the time of completing his task. So the sketch made of the suspect looks more like a lantern-jawed alien than a real person. Secondly, the witnesses claimed that the man was in his late thirties. Witnesses are notorious for getting ages wrong and the police dismissed too many possible subjects out of hand because they didn't fit the profile."

Several witnesses stated that the man was seen dressing the children prior to leaving the beach. The children's parents said that the kids, especially Jane, were very shy and unlikely to speak to a stranger. This later led police to theorize that the children had met the man in question prior to the date of their disappearance and had grown to know him over a period of several weeks.

The blond man and three children were seen leaving the beach together at 12:15pm, after the children purchased several pastries and a meat pie from a local vendor with a $1 bill, an amount of money that they did not have when they left their home that morning.

A wrench was thrown into the investigation when a postman, who knew the children and was on friendly terms with them, reported that he saw the children around 3:00pm that afternoon walking away from the beach and in the direction of their home in Somerton Park. He stated that he exchanged greetings with the young children and that they seemed to be in good spirits. In particular, the postman said that he say the children were "holding hands and laughing" as they walked down the road alone, with no blond companion in sight. Police later said that they believed the postman was mistaken about the timeline and that he most likely saw the children walking some time before noon.

Several months later, a woman in a nearby neighborhood contacted police and told them that she had seen a man with two girls and a young boy enter an abandoned house on her street. She also reported seeing the young boy walking away from the house before he was roughly grabbed by, and returned to the house with, the older man. She never saw the man or children again.

"The response from the public was overwhelming," Orange said. "People drove from miles away to aid in the search. They combed the beach and drained part of it all to no avail. They found nothing, not a trace."

The police were quickly able to eliminate drowning as the cause of the children's disappearance as a result of several witnesses saying that they saw the children leave the beach around 12:15pm. Furthermore, all of the children's belongings were missing, lending further support to the theory that they left the beach. After speaking with the parents, the police were able to identify seventeen different items that were carried by the children that day, providing a list of items that could be used to identify their remains or whereabouts. However, the police's continue efforts continued to prove fruitless.

The Psychic Circus

On November 8, 1966, nearly a year after the children's initial disappearance, an internationally-renowned psychic from the Netherlands, Gerard Croiset, was flown to Australia to investigate the case. His presence caused a whirlwind of media coverage in Australia and across the world. After making a series of outlandish and ever-changing claims, Croiset claimed that the children were buried underneath a warehouse just minutes away from the children's school.

"I appreciate him (Gerard Croiset) coming out to find the children," Jim Beaumont said. "But I don't believe what he said. I don't believe the children are dead and will continue to believe until given evidence that proves otherwise."

The building, which was under construction at the time of their disappearance, was eventually razed and excavated after the owners raised $40,000 for the project as a result of public pressure. No evidence of the children or their belongings were ever found.

"The press and police followed Croiset around everywhere," Orange said. "He was an obvious con artist but they were desperate. They had nothing."

A Series of Letters

Beginning in 1968, the parents of the three children began to receive a series of letters which rekindled hope in the idea that their children may still be alive. Postmarked from Dandernong, Victoria, the series of letters claimed to be written by Jane, the eldest daughter. She claimed to be under the supervision of a man and in good health and care, saying

Dear Mum and Dad,

We had a beautiful lunch today...The man is feeding us really well. The man took us to see The Sound of Music yesterday.

Police officers believed the letters to be from Jane after comparing them to examples of her handwriting and, as far as 1981, the Sidney Morning Herald produced analysis from handwriting experts claiming that the letters were actually from the missing child.

Following receipt of the letters supposedly sent from Jane, the parents received a letter from a man claiming to be in possession of the children. He said that he was willing to hand the children over to the parents at a specific time and location. The Beaumonts arrived at the appointed time and location with an undercover police officer but no one showed. They later received a letter from the same man claiming that he saw the undercover police officer arrive with the parents and that he would now keep the children, ending any hope of a peaceful exchange.

In 1992, following another investigation and remarkable achievements in fingerprint technology, authorities identified the author of the letters as a local man who was just a teenager at the time of the hoax. He reportedly wrote and mailed the letters as "a joke."

False Closure

Then, in November 2013, South Australian police received an anonymous tip claiming that the children were buried underneath a warehouse located in North Plympton. Although radar identified "one small anomaly, which can indicate movement or objects within the soil," no evidence was ever found.

The Suspects

Bevan Spencer von Einem

Bevan Spencer von Einem has long been considered the prime suspect in the disappearance of the Beaumont children. Einem was convicted of the July 1983 murder of fifteen-year-old Richard Kelvin, son of a popular news reporter, in 1984. Police have long suspected Einem of working with a series of accomplices and of having committed other abductions and murders.

In 1983, a police informant known as "Mr. B" told police that Einem claimed to have taken three children from a beach to perform medical "experiments," claiming that he performed "brilliant surgery" on the three children before accidentally killing one of them. Following the child's accidental death, the informant stated that Einem claimed to have killed the other two children and buried them in an open field outside the city of Adelaide.

Einem did bare some resemblance to the descriptions of the tall blond man given to police following the disappearance of the Beaumont children and was known to frequent Glenely Beach to spy on people in the changing rooms. He was also noted as having an obsession with children.

Einem worked as an accountant and lived with his mother. There were rumors that he was part of a ring of Adelaide professionals who shared a "hobby" of kidnapping, drugging and raping boys.

"Einem did match the description of the police sketches," Orange said. "And he did like to frequent the same beach. He seemed more interested in young teenage males as his list of known victims would indicate. Einem was a homosexual who picked up hitchhikers with his transvestite friend where they would engage in a "rough trade" style of sex. He would take photographs of his victims as a keepsake. The three young children would seem to be outside of his modus operandi."

However, Einem was significantly younger than the suspect described by witnesses; Einem was around 20 years old at the time, while the description of the suspect placed him in his late 20s. But, in 2007 local police officers identified a young man who looked exactly like a young Einem in Channel 7 news footage of the incident taken days after the disappearance. He remains a prime suspect in the case.

"The newly found news footage does implicate Einem in a psychological way," Orange said. "Killers often like to return to the scene of the crime. He was spotted on film, days after the disappearance. What are the odds against that?"

Arthur Stanley Brown

Arthur Stanley Brown, along with Einem, is considered to be one of two prime suspects in the abduction of the Beaumont children. In 1988, Brown, then 86 years old, was charged with kidnapping, raping, and murdering Judith and Susan Mackey in Townsville, Queensland. His first trial was declared a mistrial after the jury failed to reach a verdict in the case and his second trial was blocked because he was declared unfit to stand trial; Brown was suffering from dementia and Alzheimer's disease by this time.

He is considered one of two prime suspects in the case because of his connection to the murder of other children and because of his remarkable resemblance to descriptions of the tall blond man seen with the children at the time of their disappearance. He was also a prime suspect in the Adelaide Oval case, which involved the disappearance of Joanna Ratcliffe and Kirste Gordon.

"Brown was a known pedophile by his closest family members," Orange said. "He is alleged to have molested numerous younger relatives. He could be placed in the same area and time of the Beaumont children but nothing could be proven."

Although Brown is considered to be a prime suspect in the disappearance of the Beaumont children, the suspect in the case was identified as being in his late 30s; Brown was in his 50s at the time. Brown died in 2002 without ever admitting to the crime.

"Brown would move into a nursing home at the end of his life," Orange said. "He would die an innocent man with the courts never able to officially charge him because of his Alzheimer's."

James Ryan O'Neill

James Ryan O'Neill, convicted of murdering nine-year-old Ricky John Smith in the Australian state of Tasmania in 1975 and currently serving a life sentence for the crime, was considered as a suspect in the Beaumont children disappearance for some time. He is reported as having told several friends in the early 1970s that he was responsible for the disappearance of the Beaumont children in 1966. However, he was publicly eliminated as a suspect by the South Australian police. He remains in prison in Tasmania to this day.

"O'Neill was the subject of a documentary called 'The Fishermen,'" Orange said. "In the documentary, he is evasive about being the man behind the disappearance of the children. He is, however, at the forefront of most pundits who have studied the story. While Brown and Einem did not have charming personas, O'Neill did. He was handsome and smiley with the ability to manipulate everyone around him. He could fabricate lies at the drop of a hat so it is easy to believe that he would be able to charm the children into his acquaintance. People who knew him all described him as 'the most likable man you'll ever meet.' No one could believe that he would be capable of such an act."

Derek Ernest Percy

In 2007, the Victorian newspaper The Age published a report stating that Derek Ernest Percy, at the time the longest-serving prisoner in the southeastern Australian state, was responsible for the disappearance of the Beaumont children in 1966. Initially jailed in 1970 for the 1969 murder of 12-year-old Yvonne Tuohy, Percy was found not guilty of the crime by reason of insanity, but was nonetheless jailed "indefinitely."

He is widely considered to be Australia's worst child serial killer and is suspected of the killings of the Beaumont children, as well as the abduction, attempted rape, and stabbing of Marianne Schmidt and Christine Sharrock on January 11, 1965. In October 2014, Percy was also ruled to have abducted and killed seven-year-old Linda Stilwell in 1968. However, Percy passed away from cancer in 2013, having never admitted to any of his crimes. He remains a possible suspect in the case.

"Percy is unique in that he may have had his mother not aiding him but covering up for him," Orange said. "He is certainly one of the most sadistic pedophiles on record, his doings are unmentionable out of respect for his victims. He was in the city at the time of the Beaumont children disappearance and is probably the top suspect along with O'Neill. His mother, however, has thrown out a lot of what could have been evidence in the case."

Related Cases

Two similar cases to the disappearance of the Beaumont children attracted widespread attention in the South Australian media, and the primary suspect in the Beaumont children's kidnapping case was convicted in one case and suspected in the other.

The Adelaide Oval Case

On August 25, 1972, two young girls, Joanne Ratcliffe (aged 11) and Kirste Gordon (aged 4) went missing while attending an Australian football game. They are presumed dead. This case also received widespread attention in the South Australian media and

Bevan Spencer von Einem was considered the primary suspect in their disappearance.

Einem matched the descriptions of the tall blond man provided by witnesses in the Beaumont children's case and closely resembles the police sketch released to the public. A private police report in leaked in 1989 identified Einem as the primary suspect in the case.

The Family Murders

From 1973 to 1983, a group of men is believed to have been involved in the abduction, rape, and murder of a series of young men and male teenagers in the Adelaide area. Five teens were killed during this time period, including Alan Barnes (aged 16), Neil Muir (aged 25), Peter Stogneff (aged 14), Mark Langley (aged 18), and Richard Kelvin (aged 15). All victims were abducted and subjected to extended bouts of torture and physical assault, including sexual assault and medical experimentation.

Bevan Spencer von Einem was convicted of the abduction and murder of Richard Kelvin 1984 and is currently serving life in prison in Port Augusta prison. In 1990, he was also charged with the murder of Alan Barnes and Mark Langley, but key evidence from the Richard Kelvin murder was ruled inadmissible in the trial. Following the ruling against this key evidence, the prosecution dropped these charges against Einem on December 21, 1990.

Although Einem was the only member of this group to be convicted, and four out of five of The Family Murders remain unsolved, law enforcement officials believe that Einem was part of a white-collar group that preyed on young children. He remains the prime, and only living, suspect in the disappearance of the Beaumont children.

Impact on the Parents

Jim and Nancy Beaumont continued to hold out hope of finding their children for several decades after their disappearance. In fact, the couple continued to live at the Somerton Park home, at 109 Harding Street, that they shared with their children for nearly two decades, hoping that the children would return home someday. Nancy Beaumont was reported as saying that it would be "dreadful" if the children returned to the home only to find that their parents had moved.

"The Beaumonts left the rooms of the children untouched," Orange said. "Every toy, every book even the bed was left exactly as the children had left them."

The couple were never considered as suspects in the case and cooperated with the police at every turn in the investigation, including working with the police and searching in vain every time a new lead developed in the case over the next several decades.

According to The Age, the parents "have since separated, but still live in Adelaide." The stress and sorrow that resulted from their children's abduction, combined with the constant new leads and media attention is said to have contributed to the failure of their marriage.

Jim, in particular, is said to still be suffering from intense and inconsolable grief every time a new development is reported. Nancy was also reported to have suffered extreme grief and horror when, in 1990, several Australian newspapers released computer-generated images of what her children would look like after aging several decades. She reportedly refused to look at the pictures.

"Jim was a little bit stronger than Nancy," Orange said. "He would address the media more than she did. But they both suffered terribly for the rest of their lives into their eighties. They would spend over fifty years wishing for their children's return, getting false hope after false hope, one false lead after another which would all ultimately turn up nothing. It was a horrific cruelty."

Lastly, Jim and Nancy have largely been seen as sympathetic and pitiable figures in the Australian media and in society at large. Although their actions may seem reckless or irresponsible by today's standards, Australian society was viewed as extremely safe in the 1960s and their policy of allowing a child to supervise their younger siblings both in the home and in public was practiced by a large portion of Australian parents.

Impact on Australian Society

The disappearance of the Beaumont children became an overnight sensation in Australia, led to one of the largest police searches in the country's history, and remains the most famous missing persons case in the country. Prior to this incident, Australia was largely viewed as one of the safest societies on the planet and children were allowed to roam freely, doors remained unlocked at all times, and there was little fear of strangers. All of that changed overnight.

"Australia lost its innocence with the disappearance of the Beaumont Children," Orange said. "For three young children to disappear was unheard of. The city where they grew up was a dignified place, a safe place. But it was all an illusion that went away the day the children went missing."

During the initial search for the children, Jim Beaumont went on national television to appeal for their safe return. His heartfelt address to the nation had a lasting impact on the parents and children who watched his plea. Hundreds of viewers called into the station to offer tips and Australian police report that hundreds of tips continue to come in every year to this day. His image on national television continues to serve as a warning for those who believe in the incorruptibility of their fellow citizens and in the safety of their country.

"A lot of people today will blame the parents for letting them go on the bus alone," Adelaide resident Rachel Harding said. "But times were different back then. Back then kids would walk to school by themselves. Kids were told not to talk to strangers. The Beaumonts did tell their children to not talk to children. But child molesters are cunning monsters. My guess is that he may have stolen the eldest child's purse then conned them into seeing him as their benefactor. They would not have had money to get home then along comes this "blonde man" who offers them money. Buys them food and promises to take them home."

Children who came of age in Australia during the 1960s have remarked that there was a definite culture shift following the Beaumont children's disappearance, often describing a "before" and "after." While children were once allowed to roam freely and interact with strangers, Australian parents have since altered their style of parenting and curtailed the amount of freedom offered to young children.

"It was the type of case where we believe there was a lone offender," Australian police detective Des Bray said. "It isn't the type of crime where one would go around bragging about. But we do hope that he told someone and that somebody knows something."

If the Beaumont children are alive today, they would all be in their 50s and would have lived through years of hearing their names and story broadcast on national television and reported on breathlessly in national newspapers. Despite the vast amount of information we have on the case, their fates may never be known with any certainty.

Both Jim and Nancy Beaumont are still alive, and as of this writing they are ninety and eighty-years old respectively. The anonymous tips and false hopes continue to come in today as they did over fifty years ago.

THE STRANGE DISAPPEARANCE OF PATRICIA MEEHAN

NATHAN NIXON

Patricia Meehan Disappearance

The story of Patricia Meehan is a very strange and puzzling one. She seemingly disappeared into the night with little reason. The case has remained unsolved since 1989. With few witnesses, the full events are sketchy at best. What is well known about this case is that our culture has seemingly thought of every possible scenario to explain what happened to her. To understand and possibly solve the case, understanding the person that Patricia Meehan was is of paramount importance.

Patricia Meehan was never afraid of change. Her path of life took her all over the United States and to nearly every type of region. She was born on November 1, 1951 in Pittsburgh, Pennsylvania. She lived a typical life. She was said to have been "the perfect child" by her loving parents and by all who knew her. She had great ambition to see the world and to attack life with a smile. Socially she was on the same level as her peers. When she decided to attend college in Oklahoma City, Oklahoma, no one was really surprised. That was who Patricia was. That is exactly what she did.

She studied early childhood development and earned her degree in four years of college study. Again, she was living the American dream and successfully setting up a future to thrive. She made many friends in Oklahoma, even though it was a foreign place to a young woman from Pittsburgh. She took up a career in early childhood caregiving in Oklahoma and thrived in the profession for nearly 10 years. She was unhappy, or perhaps, unfulfilled in her work. She sporadically spoke with her family and a few friends from back home in Pennsylvania at the time. People knew Patricia to take risks. She was never afraid to change her outlook if it meant a new adventure or perhaps a new challenge lay ahead. In 1985, she made a major life change that would, effectively, lead to her ultimate disappearance.

She had informed her parents in the years prior that she wanted to become involved in animal care. She made this a reality when she moved to Bozeman, Montana in 1985. She moved alone. Patricia was not married and had left her simple, safe life behind in Oklahoma to pursue a career as a ranch hand. While this major career shift was motivated to start a happier life, it ultimately didn't always pay the bills. She worked numerous odd-jobs in the industry and could successfully make ends meet on her own. She continued this new lifestyle for four years in Bozeman, Montana.

The last person that can be fully confirmed to have seen Patricia Meehan alive was her landlord. Meehan's landlord reported to police investigators later that she seemed much more hyper than normal. This struck the landlord as extremely odd for the normally mellow, collected Patricia. Nonetheless, there were absolutely no problems between the two in any way. Patricia always paid her rent and was an "overall great tenant" to have.

The evening of April 20, 1989 is one of great speculation as to what really happened. The testimony of Peggy Bueller has always been a key component to the theories of Patricia's disappearance.

At approximately 8:05 P.M. Peggy Bueller and her father were traveling west bound on Montana State Highway 200. They were passing through the tiny town of Circle, Montana. To their surprise, they could see a set of vehicle headlights heading straight at them up ahead. A vehicle heading east was driving on the wrong side of the road. Peggy managed to swerve onto the shoulder and avoid a head-on collision with the opposing driver. The car that had been following behind Peggy was driven by an off-duty police dispatcher named Carol Heitz. Unfortunately for Carol, she was not able to swerve and avoid a collision.

Peggy Bueller had pulled over and gazed in her rear-view mirror in time to see the collision with the car driven by Carol Heitz. Thankfully, no injuries occurred in the accident. The story is very odd and somewhat eerie from this point. Just after impact, Carol Heitz emerged from her vehicle unharmed. She was shook up, but suffered no major injury. Being a police dispatcher, her first concern was for the other driver. The car that was traveling east bound was driven by Patricia Meehan. Patricia was next to emerge from her car after the impact. She stood in the middle of the road, and proceeded to slowly approach the car of Carol Heitz. According to Heitz, Patricia Meehan did not utter a single word. "She approached me calmly and silently," Heitz reported. "She seemingly stared directly through me from the moment she began to approach me."

Peggy Bueller remained in her vehicle and observed what was taking place. What she observed was "one of the strangest acts" she had ever seen. Peggy and Heitz agree that Patricia climbed over a fence just off of the road after she passed by Carol. She took only a step after getting over the fence and turned back around to stare upon the accident. She made no noise or any sort of expression. She stood there for at least two minutes. Heitz described Meehan as someone who seemed to be observing the accident scene rather than someone who had been involved in the accident. After a few short minutes, Meehan turned around and walked into a secluded Montana field into the pitch dark night. This was the last confirmed sighting of Patricia Meehan. By the time police arrived to sort out the accident, the whereabouts of Patricia were unknown. Peggy and Carol gave the exact same story in separate interviews with investigators. As eerie as the accident had unfolded, it had ended quietly and abruptly. Patricia Meehan was officially gone.

Peggy Bueller quickly drove into town when Patricia disappeared into the night. Her father stayed with Carol Heitz at the scene of the accident. Peggy reached a phone within ten minutes and alerted the authorities. When police arrived, an extensive search of the field where Patricia was seen walking away to turned up nothing. It only took police 15 minutes to identify the then mystery woman as Patricia Meehan after they ran the license plate of the vehicle. She was a registered member of the Bozeman, Montana community and had no criminal record. This was shocking to police who had assumed the woman left due to the fact that police would be arriving to the scene to investigate the accident. This posed the burning question that is still unanswered of why this woman would leave the scene of the accident if she had no criminal record.

Police made efforts to investigate the field immediately following the accident. Police discovered a tennis shoe about a mile into the field that had been accompanying a trail of footprints. The shoe matched what would have been the approximate size of the foot of Patricia Meehan. Oddly enough, the tracks seemingly disappear. Due to darkness, the investigation was suspended until the following morning of April 21. When police arrived to further check for a trail, the footprints led to nothing. The terrain had an influence in this as well as the fact that the actual shoe prints were gone, likely due to Patricia going barefoot at this point in her walk. Police had no leads.

There were two major theories that investigators had arrived at to this point. The first was the most likely. They believed that Patricia had hitchhiked from a small rural road in the area with a trucker. This could obviously not be confirmed, however the lack of a body, further clothes or footprints, as well as a lack of any whereabouts in surrounding cities points to this to be the likely case. The second theory they had suggest that she stowed away in a hay truck in the area and accomplished the same thing. This proved later to be unlikely as no hay trucks were confirmed to be in the field or in the immediate area.

The Meehan family arrived to Montana from Pittsburgh in the day following the accident. They distributed over 2,000 missing person flyers in the surrounding Montana towns and provided police with valuable information. The flyers turned up numerous calls, however none of these would lead to finding Patricia. Over 500 local volunteers searched the mountainous terrain around the accident site in an effort to possibly locate Patricia. For days, people walked the area. Some even brought dogs to perhaps catch a scent trail. These searches turned up absolutely nothing. There was no evidence of human activity in the mountains, and there were no evidence of a body or struggle in the surrounding area. Patricia had seemingly disappeared without a trace after taking a path into a secluded field. Perhaps the events in the days and weeks prior could shed some light into who Patricia was and things she had been recently going through.

The Meehan family revealed to police that Patricia had been going through some dark times in the past couple of months. Patricia was somewhat at a dead end and was feeling lost. She had asked her parents if she could return home in an effort to get back on track. Her parent's agreed, but only if she see a psychologist leading to coming home. Patricia agreed. She was diagnosed as suffering from depression. Ironically, she had an appointment with her psychologist the morning after the accident on April 21. She obviously never made this appointment.

Police also were suspicious as to why Patricia was even in this part of the state anyway. She had an appointment in Bozeman, Montana for the next morning. Bozeman was where she was living. The direction of travel she was taking at the time of the accident was in the opposite direction of Bozeman. Investigators asked the Meehan family if they had any idea where she may be going or what she was doing in this remote part of Montana. They had absolutely no idea. It was evident to police that she had no intention of returning to Bozeman to make her appointment the next morning. But could there be more to this part of the story?

The Meehan family had a roll of film developed that had been found in Patricia's car the night of the accident. The film was fully used. There were numerous pictures of nature. Beautiful countryside and the secluded area that Patricia loved. There were also numerous pictures of animals, specifically horses, that Patricia had devoted her life to in the recent years. Patricia's family stumbled across one picture that was quite alarming. A random picture that Patricia had taken in front of a mirror.

She had a very confused look on her face and seemed lost. Investigation of the picture by mental professionals led some to believe she could have been suffering from amnesia. This could obviously not be proven, but would go further in explaining the odd behavior she displayed that night. Some of the investigators pointed to this as a possible reason that she was driving away from Bozeman and was 300 miles away from home. Could she simply have forgotten how to get home? Could her mental health had gotten that bad?

Patricia had been driving on the wrong side of the road and made no effort to swerve. Police drew two possible conclusions to this fact. The first was that she was so far lost in amnesia that she simply didn't think she was doing anything wrong or perhaps forgot the basic rules of driving. The second was that she was possibly trying to harm herself or had gotten so careless that the results were not clearly thought through. These are obviously speculation and will never be proven one way or the other. The mental health of Patricia was most assuredly in a low place.

The roll of film that was developed also proved something else to investigators and the Meehan family. Socially, she was in a dark place also. Out of every picture that had been developed, not one of them featured people that weren't named Patricia Meehan. This is clearly not the norm. Patricia had mentioned that she had had a few boyfriends since arriving in Montana, but nothing serious and committal. She had previously mentioned to her parents that she had become lonely and never really made any friends in her new home. This could help to explain the depression and possible mental health issues that she had developed.

Over the last 25 years, there have been over 5,000 reported sightings of Patricia Meehan. Through all of this, only 3 of those do police feel could be Patricia or are even likely to be her. In the days following her disappearance, there were some interesting leads that were generated by the public calls on the missing person flyers.

On May 4, 1989 just two weeks after the accident, a strong lead was generated out of Luverne, Minnesota. Out of all of the possible sightings, this is considered by police and those surrounding the case to be the most likely sighting of Patricia. A police officer in Luverne claimed to have seen Patricia sitting in a Hardee's restaurant by herself. For over five hours, she was sitting in corner booth drinking water. She remained until closing time, and then proceeded to walk to a nearby 24 hour diner. Here, the officer questioned her. The woman refused adamantly to give her name. She first said that she was from Colorado, and later said she was from Israel. The major problem with all of this is that the officer could not detain her. She had done nothing wrong. However, he left without further checking to identify her. This was perhaps the best chance to obtain Patricia if this indeed was her. The officer left and where this mystery woman went next is unknown.

Another interesting sighting occurred on May 19, 1989. This is nearly one full month after the accident. A waitress at a local restaurant in Bozeman, Montana reported seeing Patricia eating there. She informed police that Patricia at in a hurry and said she had to go shopping at 9 A.M. She said she was polite, but did seem to be displaying odd behavior. Another waitress on the same shift also reported seeing her. This waitress said she was talking to herself and seemed disoriented. Patricia left the restaurant and again, no attempts were really made to investigate who she really was.

The theories that surround this case are perhaps the most interesting in the current media. If Patricia was alive today, she would be in her late 60's. This would obviously make her hard to identify in the general public. This leads to the first theory.

The first, and generally most believed theory, is that Patricia simply wanted another fresh start. She had done this in the past, albeit in a much less drastic way. She wanted a fresh start after high school, so she attended college in Oklahoma City, Oklahoma. She wanted a career change and a change of passion nearly 10 years after she started her career, so she moved to Bozeman, Montana and became a ranch hand. Many feel that she again wanted a career change and a life change at this point in her life. Turning to her parents, they gave her an ultimatum to see a psychologist before she came home. The theory suggest that she wasn't happy with her family about this. She obtained her fresh start by planning an event that would allow her to vanish into the unknown. What better place to accomplish this than a secluded highway in rural Montana where she could simply walk away.

This theory goes on further to explain that she had walked across the field and met up with someone who would drive her away. This theory doesn't sound too crazy at this juncture. The who or why is unknown, but the basis of the theory is mostly sound. Where she would have started this new life is completely unknown. But for a person who was struggling socially, not completely happy, and perhaps not enjoying the rural life as much as she had anticipated, this theory makes some sense.

The second popular theory is the more logical, medically supported theory. The collision that Patricia Meehan had was significant. While there were no injuries on the exterior, a concussion is without a doubt a possibility of this type of vehicle accident. Some believe that it was not amnesia to blame, but a concussion that would cause her to act so disoriented after the accident. The theory suggest that she exited her vehicle with a head injury and collapsed in the field shortly after beginning her walk into the night.

Montana is home to vast amounts of wildlife and has a very abstract climate. The night time temperatures in April in Montana typically are going to approach freezing. Anything under 50 degrees at altitude is going to be a severe situation for a minimally clothed, small woman with a possible head injury. The theory suggest that she was unconscious overnight and perhaps was eaten by animals, which would explain the lack of a body or any other evidence to her disappearance. It is for this reason that the theory is typically not accepted. Even with this, there would have been signs of this happening by one of the numerous volunteers or investigators in the following days.

The disappearance of Patricia Meehan has garnered national attention for the past 25 years. On November 1, 1989 the case was featured on *Unsolved Mysteries*. This would have marked the 38th birthday for Patricia.

Sightings are still reported on Patricia and a host of other in the United States. With each passing year, it is all too assuring that this case will never be solved. The lack of information on the case is puzzling. Those who choose to research the case will find that there is little information beyond the night of the accident and some significant reported sightings. All of these factors have led to a disappearance that has stumped police since that fateful night.

Patricia Meehan was an ambitious woman. She took risk in efforts to accomplish her goals and to get the most out of life. Anyone who ever knew her would say that she was a wonderful person with a positive view of the world. She loved her family dearly, and she loved her life deeply. She confidently left home to discover new opportunities on multiple occasions. It seems that life perhaps got too much for her in Montana. Maybe she just wanted to come home. Whatever the case, Patricia Meehan disappeared in April 1989, and has yet to be found. This beautiful young woman hasn't officially turned up in over 25 years. This tragic case may never be closed. A sure fact of the case is that Patricia was a sweet woman who didn't get in this situation by means of risky behavior or negative interactions. Likely, her disappearance can be attributed to a social low spot where she needed help that she didn't go through with getting. Maybe one day the truth of where her walk ultimately led will come out.

FOR MORE TRUE CRIME CLICK HERE[1]

---

1. http://www.pochepictures.com/truecrime.html

bonus:

Arlis Kay Perry was a newly married nineteen-year-old when she entered Stanford Memorial Church at Stanford University in the late night hours of October 12th, 1974. She would be found the next morning, the victim of a brutal murder in what appeared to be a ritualistic killing.

Her case has remained unsolved for the past forty-two years. Various rumors and theories abound as to who her murderer was. There is conjecture that she was the victim of the Son of Sam, the Zodiac Killer, the Death Angels and the Process Church.

The police never obtained solid leads on her case and it remains as much a mystery today as it was over forty years ago.

Who killed Arlis Perry?

EARLY LIFE

Arlis was born on February 22nd, 1955 in Linton, North Dakota to Marvin Dykema and Jean Van Beek. She usually wore glasses and had her hair straight. In the lone picture of her available online, her hair is wavy and she is not wearing glasses. This is an unfamiliar look for her and no one knows where or when the picture was taken. She was small, at 5'6" and weighing 110 lbs.

Arlis would graduate from Bismarck High School in 1973 where she was a cheerleader and a member of the Fellowship of Christian Athletes. She had a high school sweetheart, Bruce Perry, and they were both born again Christians. Bruce would be accepted into Stanford University upon graduation while Arlis would stay behind in Bismarck. She remained active in her church as a Sunday school teacher in the Bismarck reformed church.

Then she came into contact with people from the Process Church.

They were six young men that were renting a home across the street from her grandmother. Their names were Father Christian, Brother Thomas, Brother Joseph and three other men who were called "initiates."

The men tried to initiate Arlis into their religion but she soon became disenchanted with their belief system.

She realized that the were devil worshipers.

Arlis then made it a point to try and proselytize anyone who was involved in their church, leading them from Satanism into Christianity.

THE PROCESS CHURCH

The Process Cult became controversial in the early 1970s with its strong ties to the Manson family. Their belief system allowed them to worship both Christ and Satan. The church started in both Los Angeles and New York but branched out to North Dakota, as its leaders wanted the isolation of the hills and woods.

They would have meetings at the Hillside Cemetery in Bismarck and a wooded area behind Mary College. It was here that they would steal the dogs of people who lived in a nearby trailer park and sacrifice them in satanic rituals. People were complaining that they would find their dogs lying dead inside a "majick circle", their bodies badly mutilated.

MOVING TO CALIFORNIA

After graduation, Arlis would continue to participate in the Fellowship of Christian Athletes as a "huddle leader" as well as taking a job as a receptionist in a dental office. She would attend the local junior college for a year as she corresponded with Bruce Perry who was in his first year of studies at Stanford.

Bruce would return home and ask for Arlis' hand in marriage. She would accept and join him as he returned for his second year in Stanford's pre-med program.

Bruce's studies did not leave a lot of time for Arlis and she became a bit restless. She would take a job as a receptionist at a law firm to occupy her time during the day when Bruce would be away, finding work at the law firm Spaeth, Blase, Valentine, and Klein in Palo Alto.

The couple lived at the Quillen House in Escondido Village which was a campus housing unit for married couples.

Arlis got into the habit of taking nightly walks around the campus. Bruce worried for her safety and advised her not to. She stopped the practice until one night she wanted to get out of the home and mail off some letters.

DEADLY CHURCH VISIT

On October 12th, 1974 at around 11: 30 pm, Bruce and Arlis were walking on the Stanford campus. They would discover that the tire on Arlis' car had gone flat. They would have a minor argument as to who was going to take care of it. Bruce went back to the dorm and Arlis would go to the Memorial Church, telling Bruce that she wanted to pray alone.

Arlis entered and several people remembered seeing her. A security guard told her that it was almost midnight and the church was about the close up. She remained inside, however, and witnesses remembered seeing a "sandy-haired man" walk inside.

Arlis didn't return home after several hours and Bruce went out to look for her.

When he didn't find her, he called the police.

The next morning at around 05:45 am, security guard Steve Crawford would discover her body inside the church.

In Maury Terry's book, "Ultimate Evil", he described Perry's murder scene as follows:

"She was found lying on her back, with her body partially under the first pew on the left side of the alcove, a short distance from where she had been seen praying. Above her was a large carving which had been sculptured into the church wall years before. It was an engraving of the cross. The symbolism was explicit.

Arlis's head was facing forward, toward the main altar. Her legs were spread wide apart, and she was nude from the waist down. The legs of her blue jeans were placed upside down across her calves, purposely arranged in that manner. Viewed from above, the resulting pattern of Arlis's legs and the inverted blue jeans took on a diamond-like shape.

Arlis's blouse was torn open, and her arms were folded across her chest. Placed neatly between her breasts was an altar candle. Completing the desecration, another candle, thirty inches long, was jammed into her vagina. She had been beaten and choked. Death was due to her an ice pick being rammed into her skull behind her left ear, the handle protruding grotesquely from her head."

THE AFTERMATH

Security guard Crawford stated that he had locked up the church a little after midnight. He rechecked that the doors were still locked at around 02:00 a.m.

At 03:00 a.m. Perry had called the police and informed them that his wife was missing. The Santa Clara County Sheriff's went to the church and found all of the doors locked. Crawford would return to the church at 05:45 to unlock the doors and he found the west side door open.

The obvious suspect was Bruce Perry and police immediately went to brutally interrogate him.

"You knew your wife was having an affair so you killed her!"

Perry adamantly denied the questions. The police gave him a polygraph test which he passed.

Investigators would found two pieces of identifying evidence from the scene. They were able to collect a DNA sample which was found in semen near the body. The second was a bloody palm print found on one of the candles.

"It's a typical-if there is such a thing-sexual psychopathic slaying," Santa Clara County Undersheriff Tom Rosa said.

Rumors began to circulate around the campus. Some people were saying that Arlis was the victim of a satanist torture rite called the "Black Mass."

Rosa disputed the claim.

"It has no cult-like overtones," Rosa said. "It just happened to occur in a church."

There were no signs of a struggle. The detectives believed that Arlis was the victim of a "fast and sudden attack" as she entered the church around midnight.

Bruce would tell authorities that she often went there to pray when she was having problems.

SON OF SAM

Conspiracy theories would abound as the murder would go unsolved for many years. Some believe that Arlis was not murdered by a lone psychopath but by a satanic cult who stalked her from Bismarck, North Dakota.

Because of the way Arlis' body was positioned (legs spread with a candlestick in her breasts and vagina) people familiar with occult activity assumed that this was a ritualistic killing.

Fueling the speculation was some cryptic correspondence from David Berkowitz.

Berkowitz, the "Son of Sam" killer from New York City, had mentioned the Perry killing as he wrote authorities in North Dakota. He said that he had information on the killer, a man he referred to as "Manson II."

In 1979, five years after the murder, Berkowitz would send police authorities in North Dakota a book. In the margin, he had written: "Arlis Perry, hunted, stalked and slain, followed to California, Stanford Univ."

Berkowitz would claim that he was not the only person involved in the string of New York murders, hinting that he was part of a larger Satanic cult.

Detectives would later interview Berkowitz regarding Perry's murder but realized that he had "nothing of value to offer."

Those following the case, however, believe that Berkowitz should have been interrogated harder.

"Why would he make it up? He had no motive, no reason," crime writer Maury Terry asked. "He's confessed to three murders, he's not getting out."

The "Manson II" Berkowitz referred to was William Mentzer. Mentzer was suspected of being the head of the Son of Sam cult, had ties to the Manson family (although not to Charles Manson himself) and was suspected of being the Zodiac killer.

But was he responsible for killing Arlis Perry?

The answer may lie in the fact that at some point Mentzer was involved in a "hit squad" involving the Process Church. He allegedly performed assassin duties for the higher-ups who needed someone killed.

Interestingly, the serial murders of the Zodiac Killer stopped after Mentzer was in prison There were numerous parallels between the Zodiac Killer and Mentzer. Detectives believe that the Zodiac had military training. Mentzer had served in the Marines during Vietnam and killed ten people. Upon his return from the Vietnam War, the killings began in December of 1968.

The Zodiac would stab two of his victims with a bayonet style knife with rivets. Mentzer had a job where he was making rivets at a local aerospace company.

The Zodiac killer than began taunting the newspapers, sending them a diagram of a bomb while threatening to blow up a school bus. Mentzer later had a job driving a bus. He also had military training in demolition and plastic explosives. One of the survivors said that the killer spoke in a slow monotone with a drawl. Mentzer speaks the same way.

After a final letter to the press, the Zodiac mysteriously vanished in 1974.

Menzer would later be arrested for his role in the brutal murders of Roy Radin in 1983 and a prostitute/madam named June Mincher in 1984.

Radin had been shot more than twenty times in the head. Menzer would then put a stick of dynamite in Radin's mouth and blow off his face.

In the end, however, police didn't believe Menzer had probable cause to be the Zodiac killer and he would never be questioned for the death of Arlis Perry despite the rumors.

Crime writer Terry would investigate Perry's murder on his own and retrace her steps. He thinks that as many as four people were responsible for her death. He believes that the "sandy-haired" man who visited Perry at the law firm was a cult member from Bismarck, someone that she knew from the Process Church.

"She (Arlis) might have heard or seen something she shouldn't have," he said. "They may have feared she would expose them. Someone in Bismarck OK'd this, and someone had the hooks to get help on the West Coast," he said. "This was a pretty sophisticated operation."

BRUCE PERRY

Bruce Perry would complete go on to become a researcher in children's mental health and the neurosciences, becoming an internationally recognized authority in his field.

At Arlis's funeral, one of her law firm co-workers was confused when he saw Bruce. He thought her husband was a different man who had come into the workplace earlier. He witnessed her get into a "heated argument" with the man and assumed it was her husband. The co-worker described this man as "sandy-haired' which would fit the description of the man seen following Arlis into the church the night she was murdered.

Arlis would also note that there were two Bruce Perrys listed in the phone book. There is some speculation that Mentzer pretended to be Bruce Perry and had his name listed in the phone book. People from North Dakota would call and get him instead of Arlis' husband. He would then be able to finagle her whereabouts but subtly asking the family member the right questions.

This is one of the more far-fetched theories. It doesn't seem plausible that Menzer would go to the lengths of putting out a fake name and phone number just to coax Arlis' family and friends to call. Furthermore, he was a black-haired, mustachioed man who did not fit the "sandy-haired" man description.

But what is curious is that Perry's killing would be another instance of a series of unsolved murders that took place in and around the Stanford campus in the early 1970s.

A SERIAL KILLER AT WORK?

The murder of Arlis would be the fourth homicide on the Stanford campus in less than two years as well as the third incident in which the victim was a young woman out alone.

None of the murders were ever solved.

The killings started with Leslie Marie Perlov, a 21-year old Stanford history graduate who worked as a Palo Alto law librarian. She was found strangled to death on February 16th, 1973 in the foothills behind the campus. She had disappeared after leaving her workplace three days earlier.

Perlov's body would be found in a wooded gully where she had a scarf that was "wrapped tightly around her throat." There was no sign of a struggle where her body was found leading authorities to believe she walked there on her own volition.

She was not sexually assaulted but her skirt had been pulled up around her waist and her pantyhose had been stuffed into her mouth. While officers were searching for Perlov, they would find the body of Mark Rosvold, a twenty-five-year-old man out of Palo Alto. Rosvold was believed to have committed suicide the morning after Perlov was murdered. Perlov was last seen near the quarry gate of the Stanford campus, talking to a man with long blonde hair.

Seven months after the Perlov murder, physics student David S. Levine would be found stabbed to death on a walkway just east of the Meyer Undergraduate Library. The attack was estimated to have occurred between 1 and 3 a.m.

An early morning jogger would find the body of Levine. The young man had been stabbed fifteen times in the back and the side.

Like the rest of the murders, there had been no sign of struggle. The detectives believed that the young man was taken by surprise. Levine's empty wallet remained in his pants pocket and they ruled out robbery as a motive for the murder.

Levine was a straight-A student and called brilliant by his fellow students.

San Francisco Mayor Joseph Alioto believed that the murders were the work of a cult called the "Death Angels" who were suspects in the "Zebra" killings in San Francisco. Three months after the murder of Levine, a slaying took place on the UC Berkeley campus that was also rumored to be the work of the "Death Angels."

The Death Angels were a genocidal Black Muslim faction who mostly killed white people from October 1973 to April 1974. They were compromised of four black men: Manuel Moore, Larry Green, Jessie Lee Cooks, J.C.X Simon. The group committed at least 15 murders according to Wikipedia. Author Clark Howard estimates the group to be responsible for as many as two-hundred seventy deaths.

The Death Angeles would use .32 caliber pistols to shoot their victims point blank, however. They would take people by surprise but there were not any instances where they used strangulation or a knife for the initial attack as was the case for Perlov and Levin.

On March 24th, 1974, Janet Ann Taylor was strangled while hitchhiking to her La Honda home after visiting a friend on the Stanford campus. Her body was found early the next morning in a roadside ditch. Taylor was twenty-one years old and the daughter of former Stanford athletic director, Chuck Taylor.

Detectives would later concede that there were "similarities" between the Perlov and Taylor murders.

Both would be strangled although Taylor would be choked by hand instead of a scarf. Neither were sexually violated.

Both were barefoot when their bodies were found and wearing raincoats. Neither of the purses were on the person when their bodies were found.

"We really don't know who we're looking for," Sheriff's Inspector Rudy Siemssen said after the Taylor killing. "We have no motive. She apparently had no money in her purse, although you could speculate that robbery was a motive. It's a rough one."

WHO KILLED THEM?

None of the unsolved Stanford murders seem to be connected in terms of the method of killing. But, on the surface, they all were senseless and without motivation.

In the case of Arlis, there is mere speculation because of her conversations with the Bismarck Process Cult. The rumor is that someone from the cult, a leader or ordered assassin, came out to California because she tried to convert their members to Christ.

What is curious about the case is how the body was positioned. Arlis' pants were moved but placed on top of her body. The pants were positioned legs up, across her calves and her legs were spread apart. Her arms were in a crucifix position and the altar candle was shoved in her vagina.

Looking at her body from above, she was positioned in the Mason's symbol of Freemasonry. So this suggests that her murder was the work of someone involved in the Freemason cult or someone who was trying to make it look as if there was Freemason involvement.

It also appeared that Arlis may have known her killer. Her meeting with the "sandy-haired" man at work or the church may have been a scheduled meeting place. She was a devout Christian woman, used to doing the right thing, so it seems a bit odd that she wouldn't obey the security guard when he told her he was closing up the church.

The speculation is that she was meeting someone, probably the "sandy-haired" man. Who he was or how they came to meet is the question of the day. The problem is that the police failed to see the cult link in the killing, with some kind of warped religious undertones. How much of an evangelist was Arlis and who exactly did she speak with at the Process Cult in Bismarck?

The police were never interested in pursuing that line of thought.

There were rumors in Bismarck that well-known people were part of a satanic cult that performed all kinds of grisly rituals at Pioneer Park and the caves behind the University of Mary. One witness reported that they remembered seeing people come into town in priest's outfits. Only they weren't wearing white collars. They were wearing red collars and upside-down cross necklaces.

Jon Martinson, a former psychology professor at Bismarck State College, doesn't buy the theory that Arlis was stalked from Bismarck to California.

"I remember a lot of weird religious stories going on around here in that time," Martinson said. "Like covens dancing under the full moon and rituals taking place down by the river bottoms. But in her case, I think she was at the wrong place at the wrong time."

After Terry's book "The Ultimate Evil" came out, students around the Bismarck around began trolling around the University of Mary looking for any semblance of satanic cult activity. They found none but it became an urban legend around the town. The caves behind the University of Mary were eventually filled in.

Terry still firmly believes that Berkowitz knew something that the police didn't follow-up on. "It's very important to know that it was Berkowitz himself who raised the connection to (the University of) Mary, and he did it in late 1979 – nearly eight years before The Ultimate Evil was published," Terry said. "Nothing about the Mary

(University of Mary) ties to Arlis' death was made public until the book came out. But Berkowitz knew about cult activities there all along. And I also confirmed that rituals had been occurring there in the 1970s."

Ken Kahn was one of the detectives who flew into Attica State Prison in New York to interview Berkowitz. The Son of Sam killer remained vague and didn't fess up to any details. This led Kahn to believe that Berkowitz was simply messing with the crime writer and knew nothing of the murder of Perry or anyone else at Stanford.

Martinson and Terry remain adamant that Berkowitz knows something as he was documented to have been in nearby Minot Air Force base before he committed his own murders. Martinson showed Berkowitz a series of photographs from people who Terry believed was involved with Perry's murder. Berkowitz identified one of the men in the photo as someone he had met during his satanic cult meetings in Minot.

FOREVER COLD

Detectives were hoping that with advanced DNA technology and handprint databases they would get a lead on the who left behind the semen and bloody handprint.

To date, there are still no leads.

Arlis' parents would stay in contact with the Santa Clara Sheriff's Department for more than thirty years.

Eventually, however, the sheriffs would stop returning their calls.

Arlis Perry's murder remains unsolved.